Cockcroft, James D. The Hispanic Struggle for
Social Justice: The Hispanic Experience in the
Americas. 1994. 176p. index. illus. Watts, lib. ed.,
$14.84 (0-531-11185-7)
305.868 Hispanic Americans—Civil rights || Hispanic Americans—
Social conditions [CIP] 94-23968
Garza, Hedda. Latinas: Hispanic Women in
the United States. 1994. 224p. index. illus.
Watts, lib. ed., $14.84 (0-531-11186-5)
305.48'868 Hispanic American women [CIP] 94-30598
    Gr. 8–12. Blasting the old stereotypes of
weak, submissive, housebound women domi-
nated by macho men, these two books in the

THE
HISPANIC
STRUGGLE
FOR SOCIAL
JUSTICE

James D. Cockcroft

THE
HISPANIC
STRUGGLE
FOR SOCIAL
JUSTICE

The Hispanic Experience in the Americas

Franklin Watts
New York—Chicago—London—Toronto—Sydney

Frontispiece: Cesar Chavez, founder of the United Farm Workers union

Photographs copyright ©: UPI/Bettmann: frontis, pp. 6, 13, 14; Archive Photos, NYC: pp. 1, 4 (Hirz); Barker Texas Historical Center, Austin, Tex.: p. 2 top; New York Public Library, Picture Collection: p. 2 bottom; The Library of the Daughters of the Republic at the Alamo: p. 3 Santa Fe Railway: p. 5; Wide: World Photos: pp. 7, 9, 12, 14 top, 16; The Bettmann Archive: p. 8; Library of Congress/FSA/Jay Mallin: pp. 10, 11; Reuters/ Bettmann: p. 15 bottom.

Library of Congress Cataloging-in-Publication Data

Cockcroft, James D.
    The Hispanic struggle for social justice : the Hispanic experience in the Americas / James D. Cockcroft.
        p.   cm.
    Includes bibliographical references (p.) and index.
    ISBN 0-531-11185-7 (lib. bdg.)
        1. Hispanic Americans—Civil rights.   2. Hispanic Americans— Social conditions.   I. Title.
    E184.s75c63   1994
    305.868—dc20   94-22968   CIP   AC

CONTENTS

ACKNOWLEDGMENTS

I must first acknowledge all those Latinos concerned with social justice who have helped me over the years—Edna Acosta-Belén, Rudy Acuña, Tony Báez, Pete Beltrán, Humberto Camacho, María Canino, Richard Griswold del Castillo, Roberto Hernández, Hilda Hilgado, Tony Orendain, and so many other scholars, students, activists, farmworkers, and labor organizers.

And extra thanks to the librarians at Glens Falls' Crandall Library and SUNY-Albany's library in New York State, who once again came to my rescue whenever needed.

Above all, without the constant inspiration of my best friend and life companion, Hedda Garza, a true role model for social activism and consideration for others, it is doubtful that this book would have ever been written. Thanks again, Hedda!

INTRODUCTION

Until recently books rarely mentioned Hispanics—and when they did, it was usually as immigrants. Of course, except for Native Americans, *all* Americans are immigrants. Most wanted to come. African Americans, dragged here in chains, were unwilling immigrants. Long before the Pilgrims landed at Plymouth Rock, Hispanics were settling the South and Southwest, then under Spanish rule. As Mexican-American filmmaker Luis Valdés once noted: "We did not, in fact, come to the United States at all. The United States came to us."[1]

At the height of the exciting movements for social justice in the 1960s and 1970s, the U.S. government began using the term *Hispanic,* a synonym for *Spanish,* to describe a person of Spanish descent and fluent in the Spanish language. *Hispanic* officially replaced more pride-oriented, race-accurate terms like *Chicano* (for U.S. citizens of Mexican ancestry), *Boriqua* (for Puerto Rican), *Nuyorican* (for Puerto Ricans in New York City), *Latino,* and so on. Today, the U.S. Census Bureau and most institutions *require* the use of *Hispanic.*[2]

Spaniards are considered white, and to be of Spanish descent implies that one's color is white. In fact, few of the nation's Hispanics are truly Hispanics, that is, white descendants of white Spaniards. After centuries of Spanish rule, the children of the original Spanish conquerors were mixtures of many races. But some accept the description *Hispanic* as a way of "getting ahead" in a society that underrates nonwhite persons. Many individuals in the United States prefer to use the term *American* with their countries of national origin: Cuban American, African American, Italian American, Polish American, and so on.[3] Most Americans of Mexican descent and other Hispanics refer to themselves as simply Americans, realizing that so-called hyphenated Americans are less likely to be fully accepted by the dominant United States culture with its roots in northern Europe.[4] The very word *hyphenated* connotes something broken, something negative—in the case of a hyphenated American, not yet fully assimilated.

In this book we sometimes use the official word *Hispanic*. More often we employ the words the vast majority of Latinos themselves use: *Latinos, Dominicans, Colombians,* and so on.[5] We use these labels only out of an unfortunate necessity—and as a means of taking into account inequalities of economic and political power based on racism. Latinos, like African Americans, are three times as likely to be poor today as are white Americans.

Latinos are this nation's largest emergent "minority."[6] By the year 2030, they will likely account for a quarter of the population and whites will be outnumbered by nonwhites.[7]

It is never easy to leave one's home, perhaps never to see it again. In the period of greatest immigration, between 1885 and 1920, more than twenty million immigrants came to the United States when the country was industrializing. Employers sent labor recruiters to Europe and Mexico, and the nation's population doubled in size. In that period, 1.5 million people, or one eighth of Mexico's populace, shifted north of the border—one of the largest movements of a people in recorded history—and the number of Mexicans residing in the United States multiplied ninefold. Far larger numbers of Mexicans and other Latinos began arriving here after 1959.

Because so many Latinos are darker-skinned, they "assimilate to," or "blend in with," the dominant Anglo-

American culture more slowly than new arrivals from Europe. Not accustomed to identifying themselves as white or black, they are made to feel like "outlaws in the promised land."[8] Although they also long for a slice of the "American dream" pie, they strive more than white immigrants to maintain their own cultural heritage as a defense against combined "nativist" (anti-immigrant) and racist attacks. Geography has made it easier for them to keep in touch with their homelands. Most of their countries are so near they can literally almost reach their "hands across the borders."

Most Americans believe that white European immigrants "made it" in America. The implication is that *anyone* can succeed in "the land of the free' if they really try. The reality is that many Europeans who came to the United States in the early days of the twentieth century fared poorly. Most suffered economic hardship and social ridicule because of their "foreign" ways. Shouting "strike!" in several languages, they formed labor unions to demand better treatment. By organizing for a more decent and equitable way of life, they won some of the basic rights we now take for granted. Although left out of most history books. Latinos were exceptionally active in those early struggles for social justice, even though racial barriers excluded them from many of the benefits won.

Most of the struggles of the early immigrants were set back by a combination of racism, nativism, and armed force. African Americans were the worst off, first as slaves and then legally subjugated by "Jim Crow" segregation laws and physically attacked in race riots. White-racist lynchings of "Negroes" spread to Mexicans and Orientals. Jews were excluded for years by anti-Semitism. Slavs, Italians, Irish, and other "white ethnics" all suffered from discrimination, although for shorter periods than African Americans, Hispanics, and Jewish Americans. Strikers and their families were murdered and burned in their tents. The "melting pot" of the "American dream" then, as today, was a boiling cauldron of conflict.

To end the immigrants' labor militancy and make sure that the dominant Anglo-Saxon culture would not be watered down further, the 1924 Immigration Act set quotas on how many people could come from each country. Consequently, 86 percent of the nation's immigrants after 1924 came from northern Europe. Not until 1964, when equal access was extended to Latin Americans, Asians, and Africans, did this north European bias in immigration policy change.

The truth is that there never has been a melting pot. The United States yesterday, as today, has been populated by many nationalities and cultures. But only one culture has prevailed, and at great cost to social justice.

In a sense, all of us are, in one historian's words, "the children drawn from another history learning what it is to be an American."[9] Perhaps the one thing most of us have in common is our yearning for fair play, for economic and political democracy—in brief, social justice. As Apache chief Mangus Colorado once said, "Only people with empty heads feast while their hearts should be heavy with grief." The story of the struggles of Latinos is a story for all of us who believe that an injustice to one is an injustice to all.

The Civil Rights Movement helped bring the racism and injustice suffered by African Americans during the past centuries to the public's attention. Before the period of the 1960s however, many citizens were unfamiliar with this aspect of United States history. Down through the years, Latinos have endured their share of suffering from prejudice in the United States. Much of this Hispanic American experience is still too little known. Consequently, some readers may find that some of the contents of this book contradict the romanticized versions of the United States' treatment of Latinos. However, all the events related in this book have been thoroughly researched and documented.

1

uno

HANDS
ACROSS
THE
WATER

*Once the
United States
is in Cuba,
who will get her out?*
　　　　　—José Martí,
　　　　　the Apostle[1]

It was a "big day" for Cuban industrialist Vicente Martínez Ybor. At last his newest cigar factory was ready for its official inauguration in Key West, Florida.

A year earlier, in 1885, he had inaugurated a "planned city," today's Ybor City, near Tampa. It was a model of democracy, where all views, however "dangerous and radical," were welcomed.

Now as he approached his new factory, Martínez Ybor stopped short. Pickets blocked his path, carrying signs in Spanish: *"Huelga!"* ("Strike!").

"Why?" he asked one of the pickets, an African Cuban like many of the others.

"Because of the foreman you hired."

"What is the matter with him?"

"He's a Spaniard!"

Martínez Ybor undoubtedly understood the complaint. Many of the workers in his cigar factories were militant supporters of Cuban independence from Spain. Some had been forced to flee to Florida because of their struggles against the Spanish rulers of Cuba.[2]

Many early Hispanic immigrants to the United States, both workers and middle-class professionals, supported not just Cubans' but all the Latin Americans' anticolonial fights for national independence, economic freedom, and the abolition of slavery and racism. They shared a tragic heritage dating from Columbus's "discovery" of America in 1492. Many of America's original peoples never survived their "discovery." In Cuba, Puerto Rico, and the Dominican Republic, the first "visitors," Spanish conquerors called *conquistadores,* slaughtered most of the Arawak, Carib, and Taino Indians. In Mexico and Peru, millions of Aztecs, Mayans, and Incas were killed in battle or perished from imported diseases like smallpox.

Those who did survive were enslaved by the Spaniards. Hands were needed to dig out the gold and other riches and to build an empire in Mexico and Central America that was called "New Spain." Without enough indigenous people remaining to provide the necessary labor, the new rulers set up a lucrative traffic in slaves from Africa and brought in indentured agricultural workers from India, Java (Indonesia), and China. Since most of the Spanish settlers were male, they raped and sometimes married the female slaves. Consequently, most people from Latin America are a rainbow mixture of the many races forced to mix with the Spaniards. Like the cigar workers in Tampa, they share a common heritage of hatred of oppression and a longing for freedom.

After long and bitter struggles, some Latin Americans won their independence from Spain. Mexico won its independence in 1823, followed by the Dominican Republic in 1865, though Spain still managed to cling to Cuba and Puerto Rico.

The African-Cuban and mulatto men and women in Martínez Ybor's workforce knew that it was only a matter of time before Spain lost its hold on the remains of its empire. The problem was that a new threat to genuine independence loomed—the United States. They knew full well what had happened after the Spaniards were thrown out of Mexico—the United States had grabbed half the young republic's territory. Why would an independent Cuba fare any better?

From the outset, the founding fathers of the United States had cast their eyes over the waters to the south and across the prairies to the west. Long before the American Revolution, "New Spain" extended from Central America to today's Southwest and far West—from Texas to California. In 1786 Thomas Jefferson observed, "Our confederacy must be viewed as the nest, from which all America, North and South, is to be peopled." In 1809, Jefferson concluded that "Cuba would be naturally taken by the United States."[3] In 1823, Secretary of State John Quincy Adams formulated the then unenforceable Monroe Doctrine, which claimed the U.S. right to "protect" Latin America from European interference. Slaveholders in the deep South feasted their eyes on entire nations "south of the border" as potential slaveholding states.

Meanwhile, U.S. and British forces were helping Spain to fortify its military bases in Puerto Rico and Cuba in order to ensure U.S. and English merchants an increased trade in sugar, tobacco, rum, and, above all, slaves. There were a quarter of a million slaves in Cuba, 30,000 in Puerto Rico.

U.S. officials assumed it was only a matter of time before Cuba and Puerto Rico became theirs. President James Monroe (1817-25) wrote to his ambassador in Spain, "Cuba and Puerto Rico are natural appendages of the United States."[4]

Slaves in Cuba and Puerto Rico naturally did not want any nation or master to own them. Backed by university students, they revolted against Spain. Scattered bands of runaway slaves called *cimarrones* kept Spanish troops at bay for decades.

These events were watched closely by some of the first Cubans and Puerto Ricans living in the United States. Cuban patriot émigrés in Philadelphia as early as the 1820s were publishing a pro-independence newspaper, *El Habañero*.

U.S. officials, traders, industrialists, and slaveholders may have set their sights on Cuba and Puerto Rico, but miles of ocean intervened. It was far easier to acquire northern Mexico, today's southwestern United States. The area was sparsely settled, poorly guarded, and easily accessible by land. By 1820 today's Texas was already occupied by thousands of U.S. settlers who had fled the 1819 economic depression in the States and brought their slaves with them. In 1826, President John Quincy Adams sent his diplomats to the newly independent Mexican government and offered to buy Texas from Mexico for $1 million. His successor Andrew Jackson quintupled the offer.

The Mexicans weren't interested. Instead, they abolished slavery in 1829 and prohibited further U.S. immigration. Shocked, U.S. immigrants rebelled. Because Mexico now offered safe haven for runaway slaves, white "Texans," outnumbering Mexican *"Tejanos"* by six to one, viewed the Tejanos as pro-black and therefore inferior.

The doctrine of Manifest Destiny proclaimed that it was the God-given "destiny" of the United States to populate and occupy the entire North American continent. The white Texans believed that the nineteenth-century doctrine of Manifest Destiny gave them the right to take Texas. Without the official permission of the U.S. government, they seized the area.

Mexican general Antonio López de Santa Anna, who had fought the Spaniards to help win independence for his country, marched his poorly armed, exhausted, and hungry troops into San Antonio in 1836 to defend Mexican soil. Well-armed Texan soldiers battled Mexican soldiers at Fort Alamo—and lost.[5]

"Remember the Alamo!" became an American battle cry. On April 21, 1836, Sam Houston's paid mercenaries, called filibusters, attacked Santa Anna and his soldiers during the siesta hour and slaughtered hundreds. The Mexicans who surrendered "were clubbed and stabbed. . . . Texan riflemen knelt and poured a steady fire into the packed, jostling ranks."[6] Santa Anna signed away what was now the Lone Star Republic.

In 1845, Texas was admitted to the union as a state. Mexico broke diplomatic relations with the United States, and the following year President James K. Polk ordered the invasion of Mexico. Congressman Abraham Lincoln and Senator John C. Calhoun denounced the U.S. aggression. Future Civil War general Ulysses S. Grant called the Mexican War "one of the most unjust ever waged by a stronger against a weaker nation."[7] So widespread was opposition that the U.S. Army experienced its highest rates of desertion in any war before or since. A group of recent

Irish Catholic immigrants, who had fled the potato famine and British colonialism only to be drafted, deserted the Protestant general Winfield Scott to form the "Saint Patrick's Battalion" and fight on the side of their Mexican Catholic "brothers."[8]

Mexico City fell in 1847. The 1848 Treaty of Guadalupe Hidalgo legalized the conquest of half of Mexico's territory. The lands that were taken contained "rich farmlands and natural resources such as gold, silver, zinc, copper, oil, and uranium, which would make possible . . . [an] unprecedented industrial boom."[9] In 1854 the Gadsden Purchase added additional mineral-rich territory, now part of southern Arizona, to the United States.

Meanwhile, the independence struggles in the Caribbean continued. Fresh from the conquest of Mexican territory, President Polk tried to buy Cuba from Spain but failed. His secretary of state, James Buchanan, railed: "We must have Cuba. . . . Cuba is already ours, I feel it in my finger ends."[10]

U.S. slaveholders backed three unsuccessful invasions of Cuba by Narciso López, a Cuban who wanted his country to rid itself of Spanish rule and become part of the United States. Then, in the late 1850s, Southern military adventurer William Walker, cheered on by U.S. newspapers, pronounced himself president of Nicaragua, Honduras, and El Salvador. He relegalized slavery and made English the "official language." In years of bloody warfare, British soldiers and local guerrilla fighters fought off Walker. Refugees fled to Mexico and the United States. They felt relieved and proud when a Honduran firing squad ended Walker's career.

Since the 1840s, and especially after the Civil War, U.S. investors had been flocking to Latin America. In Cuba, the Dominican Republic, and Puerto Rico, they soon owned railways, telegraph, and gas-lighting companies, steam-operated refineries, mines, and trading firms. They treated "their" dark-skinned workers with disdain.

After all, were they not the "superior race" carrying out their Manifest Destiny?

During the 1850s, Cuban exiles published the New York City newspaper *El Mulato,* championing the abolition of slavery everywhere. By 1865 antislavery exiles in New York City were organizing the Republican Society of Cuba and Puerto Rico. They linked up with pro-independence elements in their homelands and émigré tobacco workers in Key West and Tampa, Florida.

In Puerto Rico, Dr. Ramón Emeterio Betances learned in 1868 of a new U.S. offer to Spain to buy Puerto Rico and Cuba and responded by giving his famous Grito de Lares ("Yell of Lares"), proclaiming the "First Republic of Puerto Rico" and abolishing slavery. Spanish troops crushed the insurrection, but the strength of the Puerto Rican opposition frightened Spain. It tried to stem the rising tide of revolt by offering concessions, promising to abolish slavery and to hold a vote on the issue of local rule. For a while, the trick worked.

While the Spaniards were calming things down in Puerto Rico, they had their hands full in Cuba. Landowner Carlos Manuel de Céspedes had freed his slaves and issued the Proclamation of Yara. This started Cuba's so-called "Ten Years War" for independence (1868–78). (It is called by most Cubans the "Thirty Years War", 1868–98, because war broke out again from 1895 to 1898. Spain was defeated in 1898 in the Spanish-American War.) In 1876, Céspedes's son became the first Cuban mayor of a U.S. city, Key West.

At that time Dominicans, Puerto Ricans, and Cubans supported one another in their fights for social justice. In the United States the political exiles united their forces. They held meetings and raised money for the dark-skinned Cuban independence fighters, known as the Mambises, who ambushed Spanish outposts, aimed their rifles at local officers and slaveholders, and forced them to free all the slaves in the 1880s and early 1890s. Their appeals to the U.S. government for help for the cause of freedom fell on deaf ears. The United States blocked Colombia's "Pan-American" plan that called on nineteen American republics to recognize Cuba's right to independence, and the struggle continued.

The Cuban guerrilla fighters relied heavily on the support of exile communities, especially the tobacco workers in Florida and middle-class professionals in New York. By 1892 most of the exiles rallied to the cause of the Cuban Revolutionary Party (PRC), founded by writer José Martí, labor unionist Carlos Baliño, and others.

Baliño, a socialist, published Tampa's newspaper *La Tribuna del Pueblo* ("The People's Tribune"). He represented cigar workers at the 1886 Knights of Labor convention, one of the first major labor union events in U.S. history. The Florida tobacco workers had fought for years to unionize—winning and losing strikes, seeing their unions rise and fall.

In Florida's cigar factories, African-Cuban and mulatto men and women, joined by radical exiles from Spain and Italy and a few Sephardic Jews, had created a highly cultured environment hospitable to diverse nationalities, races, and political viewpoints. They hired "readers" *(lectores)* to alleviate their boredom. While rolling cigars they listened to news stories from radical Havana newspapers like the anarchists' *El Productor* ("The Producer"), as well as poetry, short stories, and novels. The anarchists were prolabor egalitarians who, unlike Baliño and the socialists, believed a fair society would have no government at all. Anarchists and socialists were drawing a sizable following among the nation's millions of newly arriving immigrants.

José Martí spent fourteen years in exile from Cuba (1881–95), most of them in New York City as a correspondent for Latin American newspapers. He had an uncanny ability to unite Cubans and other Latinos from different social classes and with different political philosophies—in his words, "With all, and for the good of all."

Using funds contributed by tobacco workers, Martí launched New York's pro-PRC newspaper *Patria* ("Fatherland"). Its editor was Sotero Figueroa, an African Puerto Rican. As PRC head, Martí rejected demands by moderates and white Cubans that socialists and African Cubans be excluded. Martí helped Figueroa and African Cuban Rafael Serra found the Cuban exiles' *La Liga* ("The League") for the education and advancement of African Cubans.[11]

Martí feared U.S. military intervention in Cuba. "Once the United States is in Cuba, who will get her out?" he asked. He blamed the U.S. government for refusing arms to Cuban exiles, accusing it of violating its own "Charter of Liberties" by stretching "the limits of its power" to act "against the will of the people."[12]

Unable to stay away from the battles at home, Martí returned to Cuba and was killed leading a charge against Spanish soldiers in 1895. He became known as "the Apostle," and remains a beloved champion of independence. His name and writings are well known to almost all cubans as well as many other Latin Americans. His verses, including the words "With the poor of the earth I wish to cast my lot," make up Cuba's most popular song, the world-renowned "La Guantanamera."

In 1896, President Grover Cleveland warned Spain that, should she lose Cuba, "higher obligations" would fall upon the United States.[13] He cited U.S. business investments in Cuba worth $30 to $50 million.

By 1897, Cuba's highly motivated 4,000 guerrillas were routing Spain's 200,000 soldiers. Spain attempted to hold on to Cuba and Puerto Rico by offering the islands autonomy under Spanish sovereignty. Puerto Rico accepted and was admitted into the Universal Postal Union as a self-governing legal entity. Spain agreed never to cede or sell Puerto Rico without the consent of its inhabitants. Cuba's victorious guerrillas refused the autonomy compromise.[14]

The people of the United States were divided on the correct policy to follow in Cuba. The half-million strong Anti-Imperialist League, founded in 1898 by respected intellectuals like Harvard philosopher William James, opposed intervention as "imperialist." Women, African Americans, and Hispanics flocked to the League's rallies. Most businessmen feared another black-ruled Haiti would be born if Cuba's mostly black guerrillas took over an independent government.

Then, on a February night in 1898, the U.S. battleship *Maine,* presumably safe in Havana's tightly guarded harbor, mysteriously blew up. "Remember the *Maine!*" trumpeted U.S. jingoistic newspapers. The U.S. National Archives' files on the sinking of the *Maine* are still ruled "off limits" to historians. Some believe the ship was deliberately blown up by U.S. agents in order to justify U.S. intervention in Cuba.

The day before President McKinley delivered his war message to Congress, he received a cable from the American Ministry in Madrid advising him that Spain was willing to grant Cuba's rebels autonomy or independence or to cede the island to the United States. But McKinley knew that if he accepted Spain's offer of Cuba he would still have to deal with the Cuban guerrillas. So he prayed to God and opted for war.

On April 25, 1898, the Spanish-Cuban War became the Spanish-Cuban-American War. Desertion and draft evasion were proportionately higher than in any other U.S. foreign war since the Mexican War and until Vietnam. There were only two major U.S. battles—San Juan Hill, Cuba, and Manila Bay, the Philippines. In ten weeks Spain surrendered to U.S. forces in Cuba and the Philippines and offered to sign an armistice. No Cuban was consulted.

After the Spanish surrender in Cuba, U.S. troops invaded Puerto Rico. Spain surrendered there in October 1898. Peace negotiations in Paris, without a single Puerto

Rican present, produced the Treaty of Paris. It granted independence to U.S.-occupied Cuba and ceded Puerto Rico, the Philippines, and Guam to the United States.

Secretary of State John Hay called the 1898 war a "splendid little war."[15] Teddy Roosevelt, who based a political career on leading a charge up San Juan Hill, later acknowledged, "It wasn't much of a war, but it was the best war we had." Roosevelt was the colorful president who boasted, "I took the [Panama] Canal."[16]

As the twentieth century began, the United States not only dominated the former Spanish empire but was in direct or indirect control of the thousands of Latinos— Mexicans, Puerto Ricans, Dominicans, Cubans, Central Americans—living in newly acquired lands in the United States and abroad. Now Latinos faced new conquerors, a fact that would color their struggles for social justice for years to come.

2 *dos*

RIGHT

TO A

PIECE

OF THE

SOIL

Then said Gregorio Cortez
With his pistol in his hand,
"Ah, so many mounted Rangers,
Just to take one Mexican!"
— Mexican-American
corrido (ballad)[1]

Dressed in a wrinkled suit, the middle-aged judge of Taos, New Mexico, wiped perspiration off his brow with a handkerchief and began pawing through a stack of papers. It was a hot summer day in the year 1882. The judge pulled out a freshly written legal-size brief.

"Tony . . . uh . . . Chacón, rise and approach the bench," he ordered, mispronouncing the man's Spanish surname.

Antonio T. Chacón stood up. A short, dark-skinned older man, he wore a cowboy shirt, faded white trousers, freshly polished well-worn boots, a handmade leather vest.

"Are you Tony?" The judge scratched at his nose each time he asked a question.

Nodding and stepping forward, the man pointed out the courthouse window with a wide-brimmed straw sombrero.

"Your Honor, I am Antonio T. Chacón and, with your permission, I wish to speak."

"Very well. Proceed."

"For three centuries those lands you see out there have belonged to the individuals who till them and the communities that share them. Our customs from the Spaniards and from the Aztec and Pueblo Indians, even when we've had our disagreements, have always defined the ownership of those lands by occupancy and use."

"Do you have proof, title, deed to your ranch?" the judge snapped.

"Who needs proof, Your Honor? My name is known here. My ranch along the Arroyo Seco ["Dry Ravine"] may not be so good, it lacks water, but my ancestors have always taken good care of it."

"Proof, Mr. Chacón."

"But, Your Honor, I already delivered you the 1716 Martinez land grant of the Santa Fe Spanish Royal Garrison."

"Tony," the judge interrupted, shifting his tone to

one of a father addressing a child. "Can you pay your back taxes you owe the county?" He again scratched his nose.

"This is a new custom for us, Your Honor."

"It says here you owe more than a hundred dollars. . . ."

The judge paused to pull out another legal sheath.

"Indeed, this title shows the land belonging to one Arthur Rockford Manby, the gentleman sitting to your right. It postdates the Martinez land grant. If you can't pay your taxes, Mr. . . . uh . . . Tony, I'll have to honor Mr. Manby's title and dispossess you."

Antonio T. Chacón replaced his hat on his head and looked up at the judge sternly, raising his index finger for emphasis.

"Ever since the railroad arrived here in seventy-eight, I've watched you judges mock our rights. I've seen land grabbers, tax assessors, mine investors, and lawyers marching roughshod over our Taos-Santa Fe communities as if the Treaty of Guadalupe Hidalgo did not exist. I've figured out how your kind cheat my neighbors out of their land rights recognized by the treaty. You loan us money to pay inflated county taxes or back bills at the *bodega* ["grocery store"] or lawyer fees for these land disputes and then, when we can't meet a payment, you force us to sell our ranches for a song. But I tell you one thing, Your Honor. That is not honorable, not right. The land, it is ours."

"You're out of order, Mr. Chacón. Can you pay the taxes?"

"Your Honor, my wife, my seven children, my grandchildren, without land, how can we—"

"Can you pay?"

Silence.

"You leave me no choice but to dispossess. Bailiff, get a posse to the Arroyo Seco ranch this afternoon. Case dismissed."

The judge banged his gavel.[2]

Like most in his community, sheep rancher and corn farmer Antonio T. Chacón lost his lands to the "Anglo invaders," as he and his neighbors called the new arrivals to today's Southwest. He and his family were soon forced to work for poverty wages at the mines or ranches they once owned. Descended from mixed marriages of Spaniards and Native Americans, Chacón was one of many whose lands and labor were highly valued by English-speaking settlers expanding westward before and after the Mexican War.

When Chacón was a teenager, he witnessed a "people's revolt" against the "Anglos" taking over northern New Mexico—the Taos Rebellion. Led by a Mexican peasant and a Pueblo Indian, the rebels killed the first Anglo civilian governor of the New Mexico territory and barricaded themselves in an old church. U.S. troops smoked them out, killing about 150. Prisoners were given public whippings, and twenty-five or thirty of them were mowed down by firing squads.[3] In those times, small farmers often took up arms against wealthy landowners—one case being the white tenant farmers' Anti-Renter Movement in New York's Hudson River Valley.[4]

Over the years, Chacón had noticed how even the poorest whites turned against "his kind," calling them "greasers." Some towns in the Southwest were even called "Greaserville."[5] Chacón had watched the whites' work crews build forts to house the U.S. troops needed to make "his kind" outcasts in their own land.

The 1848 Treaty of Guadalupe Hidalgo and its protocols terminating the Mexican War supposedly guaranteed to the 100,000 Mexicans of the Southwest U.S. citizenship and their civil and property rights. But Anglo slaveholders, rail tycoons, mine investors, industrialists, ranchers, farmers, land speculators, and judges usually ignored the treaty's provisions. Even though the new arrivals were outnumbered by New Mexico's 60,000 Mexican Americans, they quickly relegated the Mexicans and Indians to the bottom of society, claiming they were "inferior," "lazy," "not like us"—in other words, not human, *the other.*

Manby's cheating of Chacón was backed up by force. Known for leading a secret Anglo society that ran an extortion racket, Manby frequently ordered his opponents beheaded. In 1929 he died the way he had lived—shot seven times in the chest and face.

Federal land grants and water reclamation projects favored railroad owners and corporate farmers. Mexican Americans and Native Americans lost more than twenty million acres. With no land to grow their food or graze their livestock, they were forced to work for the men who had taken their land. The only other choice was to starve to death.

Throughout the nation, racial violence flourished. In the South, African Americans were lynched. In the Southwest, Mexican Americans were the victims.

People like Antonio T. Chacón found various means to cope with their new problems. Some of the lighter-skinned "ricos" or wealthier Mexicans of New Mexico called themselves "Hispanos" or Spanish Americans. Trying to "pass" as Euro-American, they accommodated to the whites' takeover by becoming managers and foremen for the Anglos or bringing them into the family by arranging for their daughters to marry them. On a lesser scale, this also happened in Texas. Still other Mexican Americans lost their lives in heroic but futile individual acts of armed self-defense. At other times, such as the Taos Rebellion, there were "people's revolts." Occasionally, poor "Anglo" land squatters joined Mexican Americans in these uprisings.[6]

A particular enemy of Hispanics in the Southwest was the much celebrated "American" cowboy. The Hispanics of former northern Mexico were actually the nation's first cowboys. They herded their sheep and cattle on communal open lands, sharing the grass and the water. The Anglo cowboys believed in private property and wanted the communal lands for their own cattle. They raided the Mexican-American grazing areas, killing many Mexican Americans, raping their wives and daughters, and stealing their cattle. In short order, barbed wire was strung up to mark off the new "property" of the Anglo cowboys.

Many Mexican Americans stood up to these well-armed raiders. Later they would be folk heroes, their stories passed down through a form of Mexican folk music known as the *corrido,* which is still widely sung in parts of the Southwest and Midwest.

In the Texas Panhandle, Sostenes l'Archevêque, whose father was French and mother Mexican Indian, acquired twenty-three notches on his gun—two more than Billy the Kid—before other Mexicans executed him in hopes that Anglo raids might cease. Instead, Texas cowboys shot up some Mexican plazas and drove the Mexicans into New Mexico.

There, in the 1880s, native New Mexican Elfego Baca became a volunteer deputy sheriff. One day he dared to jail a raiding Texas cowboy, enraging the non-Mexican community. Baca then barricaded himself in an adobe and opened fire on scores of whites who attacked him, leaving several dead or wounded. The armed cowboy raids simmered down after that.[7]

Mexican Americans who fought back were labeled bandits. In the eyes of many of their neighbors, however, they were heroes. Many scholars today describe the rebels as "social bandits," because of their record of retaliation against violent injustice. Some of the most famous social bandits first appeared in California, where the 1848–49 "Gold Rush" quickly stripped the Hispanic "Californios" of both their mining rights and their lands. José María Flores led a successful guerrilla resistance in Los Angeles until he was overpowered in January 1847. Additional U.S. troops poured in, and California became a state in 1850.

Thousands of gold-hungry "forty-niners" rushed into the state, attacking any "foreigners" who got in their way. A California legislator publicly compared all Latinos to "the beast in the field . . . a curse to any enlightened community."[8] Inflamed with greed and racism, mobs of Anglo miners lynched many "foreign" miners. The first woman hanged in California was named Juanita in the press, although her real name was Josefa. English-language newspapers commonly referred to any Latino as Juan, Joaquín, or Juanita. The Los Angeles Spanish-language paper *El Clamor Público* ("Public Outcry") angrily nicknamed the Euro-American democracy "Linchocracia."[9]

The forty-niners set up their California homes on Mexican-American lands in north-central California. The Federal Land Act of 1851 required Mexican Americans "to present evidence supporting title within two years, or their property would pass into the public domain."[10] Attacked at every turn and unable to meet high lawyer fees and court costs, most Mexican Americans became impoverished second-class citizens. Outnumbered ten to one, they were pushed into the southern part of the state.

A steep monthly state tax on "foreign" miners assured the English-speaking newcomers the lion's share of California's gold. Chilean, Peruvian, Mexican, and Central American miners, who were already there or among the first to arrive, taught other gold seekers how to dig a mine shaft and pan for gold. For "thanks," they were violently pushed off their claims.

Understandably, legendary social bandits were supported and sometimes aided by the Spanish-speaking masses. They carried out frequent retaliatory robberies, and although tempting rewards were offered for their severed heads, few Latinos betrayed them.

One of the best-known early social bandits was Juan "Cheno" Cortina, a U.S. citizen who led a guerrilla war in Texas's southeastern Rio Grande Valley from 1859 to 1861. Targeting unpunished lawmen and ruffians who killed or terrorized Mexicans, Cortina and his followers fought off the local militia called the Brownsville Tigers, the Texas Rangers, federal troops, and the Mexican Army. During "the Second Cortina War" of the early 1870s, Anglo outlaws, assuming that every Mexican was part of Cortina's army, raided Mexican ranches, killing every adult male and raping the surviving females. A Texas state commissioner sent to investigate reported: "I am sorry to say a good many . . . who have been Burning and Hanging and shooting Mexicans . . . are more dreaded than Cortina."[11]

After Porfirio Díaz became Mexico's dictator (1876–1911), Cortina was jailed in Mexico City, then released and kept in exile there under close surveillance. When Cortina returned to south Texas briefly in 1890, he received a hero's welcome from Mexican Americans.

Sometimes ordinary people banded together when their meager livelihoods were threatened. In 1877, politicians and speculators seized communal salt beds in El Paso. The men and women who dug for the salt sold it to earn money to buy food for their families. With their land gone, they had nothing left. Arming themselves, they rose up against the notorious "Salt Ring." They defeated a troop of Texas Rangers before being subdued by reinforcements.

Anyone who stood up to the hated Texas Rangers, *los rinches*, became a hero in the eyes of Mexican Americans. In the early 1900s a cowhand named Gregorio Cortez killed a south Texas lawman sent to arrest him unjustly. He led *los rinches* on an amazing 500-mile chase before he was caught. He was hauled before an all-white jury, convicted, and jailed. In 1913, after years of appeals, he was pardoned. Contemporary *corridos* still celebrate him as a hero. In 1983 his story was made into a favorably reviewed film starring the Mexican-American actor Edward James Olmos. Millions of people watched it on public television in the 1990s.[12]

In New Mexico, around 1887, a militant group called Las Gorras Blancas ("the White Caps") began fending off land grabbers. The founder of Las Gorras Blancas was a district organizer for the nation's first major labor union confederation, the Knights of Labor, the same group Florida's Cuban tobacco workers supported. During the San Miguel County land wars of 1889-90 the Gorras Blancas masked their faces with white bandannas, mounted their horses, and raided jailhouses, railroad properties, and stolen landholdings. With *justice* as their watchword, they claimed 1,500 members and enjoyed the support of most of northern New Mexico's Mexican Americans.

During the borderland turmoil of the Mexican Revolution (1910-17), a small group of Mexican Americans in the Rio Grande Valley of South Texas threatened to retaliate against increased Anglo killings of Mexicans by killing white males over the age of sixteen. Their banner was the 1915 "Plan de San Diego" proclaiming the "independence" of the border states. Their "eye for an eye" words appeared to be more bluster than reality. They killed no one, but they provoked the wrath of Texas lawmen and marauders who killed and lynched 300 "suspected" Mexicans. It was then that the rebels killed twenty-one Euro-Americans.

At that time, journalist George Marvin reported "an open gun season on Mexicans along the border." Even a noted historian known for his admiration for the Texas Rangers wrote: "In the orgy of bloodshed that followed, the Texas Rangers played a prominent part, and one of which many members of the force have been heartily ashamed."[13]

The turmoil continued until 1916. In that year, President Wilson, pressured by copper-mine owners trying to end a wave of strikes by Mexican-American and other workers (see Chapter 3), federalized the National Guards of Texas, New Mexico, and Arizona. A hundred thousand guardsmen rushed to the border, finally crushing both the Plan de San Diego rebellion and the strikes.

There were some who never forgot the loss of their ancestors' land. In the 1960s that issue was raised again when Reies López Tijerina reminded the world of the broken promises of the Treaty of Guadalupe Hidalgo and led a land claim movement in the same area where Antonio T. Chacón and his neighbors had lost their lands a century earlier (see Chapter 6).

Some Mexican Americans believe that the days of Anglo invasions are not over, but have merely taken a different form. According to a 1993 report in *The New York Times*, Santa Fe has attracted so many affluent whites that "the Hispanic culture they came to embrace has become threatened by the soaring property values." A lack of affordable housing has forced Hispanics out. Their numbers have dropped from two thirds of Santa Fe's population in 1970 to less than half in the 1990s. This time there are no social bandits to rally people to the cause of the landless. Instead, new Hispanic politicians protest. City Councilwoman Debbie Jaramillo has compared the newcomers to "conquerors who did not need arms" since "big money" sufficed.[14]

3

tres

HUELGA!

("STRIKE!")

I can hire one half
of the working class
to kill the other half.
— Jay Gould,
nineteenth-century
railroad owner[1]

If you're white, you're right;
if you're brown, stick roun';
but if you're black, get back!
— Old American folksong
describing hiring practices[2]

Women, children and old men
are being driven to the Border.
Goodbye beloved countrymen;
we are being deported.
But we are not outlaws;
we come to work."
— El Deportado
("The Deportee"),
Mexican *corrido*[3]

The bones of hundreds of nameless fighters for social justice rest under the soil near the mostly deserted mining towns of the Old West. Theirs is a David and Goliath story, and their legacy is nothing less than our eight-hour working day. Only a few Mexican Americans still talk or sing about the legends that have been passed on for generations. Late at night, as people gather around a kitchen table or a campfire to strum some *corridos* on the guitar, you can almost see what happened. . . .[4]

On a sodden rain-swept day, June 9, 1903, a haunting sound echoed down the mountainside from Metcalf, Arizona—it sounded like "Whale-gah!" It emanated, like some strange spirit, from the towering peaks of the Gila Mountains against which nestle the neighboring towns of Metcalf, Morenci, and Clifton. It was punctuated by the splatter of a steady downpour that sent rivulets of copper-tinted runoff down Chase Creek into the main street of Morenci.

There, hundreds of striking miners and their families slopped through the mud carrying signs in Spanish and English demanding enforcement of Arizona's new eight-hour-day law. They heartily bellowed the chant back up the canyon: *"Huelga!"*

Claps of thunder echoed the crescendos of their voices, as cloudbursts of rain poured down in torrents. Several hundred Mexican miners from Metcalf single-filed their way down Chase Creek Canyon to join the Morenci marchers, all now shouting *"Huelga!"*—a Spanish word often heard in the West long before its English equivalent *strike.*

Ever since their participation in the 1877 nationwide railroad strike that was put down by federal troops at the cost of over a hundred lives, Mexican workers had fought for the same goals sought by other workers. Rail workers, a polyglot of nationalities, formed the backbone of America's first big labor union, the Knights of Labor.

The shooting of strikers by the hired gunmen of rail

magnates Jay Gould, William Vanderbilt, and Edward H. Harriman only momentarily deterred America's new labor movement. In 1885, rail workers, many of them Mexicans, won a major strike that threatened to spread over Gould's entire Southwest rail system.

Within a year, membership in the Knights of Labor skyrocketed to 750,000. In 1886, known as "the year of the great uprising of labor," half a million workers demanding the eight-hour day carried out 1,400 strikes nationwide.[5] The newly founded American Federation of Labor (AFL) also championed the eight-hour day. But when anti-Mexican hysteria reached new heights in the late 1880s and 1890s, white labor leaders were infected with the racist virus and expelled Mexicans from their unions.

The employers, of course, did not object. They were happy to return to their custom of paying "their" Mexicans the rock-bottom "Mexican wage," half the wages of white workers and with two or more extra hours thrown in. At the end of a dawn-to-dusk day of cutting, hauling, and laying railway ties, Mexican workers went home with fifty cents in their pockets. In the mining camps Mexicans received their paltry wages in the form of fake money called scrip, redeemable only at the company store where the prices were sky-high. Mine owner Sylvester Mowry boasted that he paid "his" Mexicans "in large part in merchandise at large profits."[6]

With the Civil War over, America was industrializing at a feverish pace. Millions of workers were needed. Even though the new factory owners and railroad men could have hired freed slaves, they preferred to recruit foreigners. Slavery's legacy of racism was hard to shake. As part of a white backlash against gains made by African Americans during the short-lived post-Civil War "Reconstruction" years, gangs of white racists, many of them members of the Ku Klux Klan, whipped or lynched "uppity" African Americans on an almost daily basis.[7]

Employers sent labor-recruitment notices far and wide. Poor people heard the word all over the world: there were jobs waiting across the ocean. Encouraged by stories of bread, freedom, and even fairy tales that told of gold-paved streets, millions of immigrants made the long journey to the United States.

Some employers thought they could control the expanding workforce by pitting different groups against one another. Boasted Gould, "I can hire one half of the working class to kill the other half." A white worker was more likely to be satisfied with low pay if Hispanics, Asians, and African Americans earned even less. Furthermore, if factories and mills were Towers of Babel, crammed with people who spoke dozens of languages, there was little danger that they could meet together to organize unions. A racial-ethnic pecking order took shape. Native Americans and African Americans were relegated to the bottom of the heap, followed by the Chinese, other Asians, and darker-skinned Hispanics. U.S.-born white workers were treated better than white immigrants; Protestants fared better than Jews. For several years Irish Catholic immigrants faced signs at factory gates that stated: "No Irish Need Apply."

With boatloads of European immigrants steaming into New York Harbor and settling in the big cities, a shortage of labor existed in the mining towns and railroad yards of the less populated Southwest. Chinese laborers had been contracted, but the Knights of Labor had objected to the use of low-wage Chinese "coolies" and persuaded Congress to pass the Chinese Exclusion Act in 1882. The Chinese were expelled from the United States.

Exempted from laws prohibiting contract labor, however, were "foreigners temporarily residing in the United States." This loophole allowed employers to rush their labor recruiters across the border to sign up Mexicans. Many were tricked into coming or forced into railway cars heading north. A Department of Commerce inspector wrote: "One is told of locked car doors and armed guards on the platform of trains to prevent desertion en route."[8]

Usually, only adult males were "recruited," saving employers the costs of educating the workers' children. The *New York Journal of Commerce* crowed over the influx of fresh muscle power in 1886: "Men, like cows, are expensive to raise, and a gift of either should be gladly received. And a man can be put to more valuable use than a cow!"[9]

Employers tried to use the Mexican workers to destroy the still-fragile union movement. Most of the new arrivals knew little or nothing about labor struggles in the United States. They did not realize that they were being imported to break strikes. This divide-and-conquer tactic succeeded all too well for a while. Enraged white workers turned on the Mexicans. As a prominent historian wrote in 1889: "There were public meetings held to urge the expulsion of the hated 'greasers' from the mines and from the country. A war of races at times seemed impending. . . . [There occurred] acts of lawless violence, including murders, robberies, and lynching."[10]

Once the bewildered Mexicans figured things out, they supported unions too. Rejected by white unions and facing the racism of many native-born workers, they began organizing themselves. In 1901, 200 Mexican construction workers struck the El Paso Electric Street Car Company and won an agreement not to hire imported Mexican scabs. In 1903, shortly before the Metcalf-Morenci strike, Mexicans won a nine-hour day and overtime pay at the Johnston Fruit Company in Santa Barbara, California. And in the greater Metcalf Sonora-Arizona border area "mining triangle" at least, Mexicans were as likely to be aggressive union organizers as strikebreakers.

During the 1903 Metcalf-Morenci strike, the Mexicans formed alliances with European-born workers. The Europeans had been mistreated by the Anglos too. In the mines, facing the same dangerous conditions, all of them living in poverty in company-run towns, some European and even a few U.S.-born workers began to recognize the futility of going along with the divide-and-conquer strategy of their bosses.

Not one of the strike leaders, though, was U.S.-born. One was a Rumanian injured in a mine accident, known as "Three Fingered Jack," or, among Mexicans, *"Mocho"* ("Crippled Hand"). More than four fifths of the 1,600 strikers were Mexican—people like Abraham Salcido, founder of the mutual-aid society *(mutualista)* that paid the medical bills and funeral expenses of its dues-paying members and now formed the core of the striking labor union.

Some newspapers in Arizona's mining towns supported the strikers. In editorials, they blamed the companies and "Eastern money" for the sorry conditions leading to the strike. Everyone knew it was the hard, low-paid labor of Mexican workers that helped fill the coffers of East Coast "robber barons" like Rockefeller, Morgan, Gould, and Guggenheim who had invested in the mines, railroads, farms, and banks of the West. For these absentee owners, the West was a giant horn of potential wealth. With enough cheap labor, that wealth could be wrested from the earth to build a vast industrial empire back east. But the word *cheap* was the key, and now the workers were demanding decent wages instead of near-starvation pay.

Other newspapers opposed the strike, the first major one by Western miners in the nation's leading copper-producing territory. Phoenix's *Arizona Republican* attempted to undermine support for the strikers by calling the action "the Mexican Affair." They listed the Mexican names of strike leaders and sarcastically commented: "All of them good American names!" The *Tucson Citizen* responded indignantly: "What's the matter with them? All of us can't be named Cochise, Sitting Bull, Billy the Kid, Murphy, Geronimo, Sims Ely, Rain-in-the-Face or Guv'ner Hughes."[11]

"Huelga!" the Mexicans bellowed.

Near the foot of the canyon trail, Captain Thomas H. Rynning and fifteen Arizona Rangers braced themselves. They had been called in the previous day for their first big "labor test." Their hands fidgeted over the stocks of their Winchesters.

"Huelga!" repeated the Metcalf miners as they broke their single file to form a phalanx at the foot of the trail and face off against the Rangers. The lawmen, a mere handful of new recruits confronting hundreds of toughened miners, clicked off the safeties of their Winchesters.

Suddenly, a rumbling wall of water came sweeping down the hillsides. The miners suddenly changed their cry from *"Huelga!"* to *"Diluvio!"* ("Flood!") Strikers and lawmen scrambled for higher ground. The flash floods and torrential downpours swept away everything in their path, killing fifty people and destroying $100,000 worth of property. Especially hard hit was the Mexican community, segregated in the West's mining towns into overcrowded hovels, nicknamed Frogtown or Jim-town by racist townspeople.

Despite the tragedy, the strike continued. The following day, armed miners seized the Detroit Company's mill and disarmed the sheriff's deputies guarding it. Martial law had to be declared. President Theodore Roosevelt dispatched federal troops, supplemented by six companies of national guardsmen—the biggest show of force since the recent Indian wars. Jeanne Parks Ringgold, granddaughter of then-Sheriff Jim Parks of Clifton, summed up the 1903 "Mexican Affair" as "the bloodiest battle in the history of mining."[12]

Eighteen strike leaders, including Salcido, were arrested, given swift trials, and packed off to jail. They did time in the territorial prison at Yuma, the notorious "Yuma Hell Hole" with its solitary confinement dungeon known as the "Snake Den."

But the 1903 copper strike was only the beginning

of labor actions sparked by Mexican and Mexican-American workers. They soon transformed the U.S.-Mexico borderlands into an area of cross-border working-class solidarity.

In Cananea, Sonora, across the border from Bisbee, Arizona, thousands of workers struck William C. Greene's Consolidated Copper Company in 1906. As in the 1903 Arizona copper strike, they demanded the eight-hour day, a minimum wage, and an end to discriminatory hiring and promotion practices.

Salcido, recently released from the Yuma Hell Hole, was back in action. He was working with poet and journalist Práxedis G. Guerrero and Ricardo Flores Magón. A year earlier Guerrero had been jailed for organizing the Obreros Libres ("Free Workers") in Morenci, Arizona. The three labor organizers were leaders of the underground Mexican political party PLM (Mexican Liberal Party), then launching armed revolts against dictator Porfirio Díaz. They and other PLM members traveled over the mining towns of Mexico and the United States helping the workers to organize and asking for aid in their struggle to bring democracy to Mexico. Flores Magón was the founder of the popular newspaper *Regeneración* ("Regeneration" or "Rebirth"). It had a circulation of 30,000 by 1906. According to a private detective hired by Díaz to infiltrate the PLM, the paper was financed largely by small donations from "common laborers."[13]

A shooting incident during the strike at the Consolidated Copper Company's lumberyard, in which three Mexicans and two Americans were killed, touched off two days of rioting and a shutdown of production. While waiting for Mexican troops to arrive in Cananea from distant garrisons, mine owner Greene requested help from his friend Captain Rynning of the Arizona Rangers.

Rynning crossed the border with 275 more-than-willing "volunteers" from nearby Bisbee and five Rangers. To the hoots and whistles of bystanders, the American volunteers marched up and down Cananea's streets, not daring to fire a shot. When Mexican troops arrived, the Americans returned to the U.S. side of the border, having spent less than twelve hours in Cananea. It took 2,000 Mexican soldiers to finally put down the strike, leaving a death toll of dozens of Mexicans and six Americans and many more wounded.[14]

Instead of backing off from their labor-organizing activities, workers everywhere, Mexicans and Mexican Americans prominent among them, redoubled their struggles for justice. Women played an important role in all of the struggles, marching on picket lines and organizing strikes and strike support groups.

Most of the names of the many Latinas who put in "triple work days"—raising their families, often holding jobs themselves, and helping other strikers—are forgotten. One of them, Lucy González, a Spanish-speaking woman of mixed Indian-African-Mexican stock, was a world-renowned labor activist all her life. She married one of the nascent labor union movement's best orators, printer Albert Parsons. Parsons and seven others were tried and convicted for the mysterious bomb explosion that triggered the 1886 Chicago Haymarket Riot and massacre of protesting workers. All were later pardoned, but not before four, including Parsons, had been hanged and a massive international protest campaign had taken place. As one labor historian put it: "Starting from almost Lucy Parsons alone, a protest movement grew until it became world-wide and included millions."[15]

The good feelings aroused by struggling alongside white workers in some of the strikes of the early 1900s encouraged Latinos everywhere to attempt to join the mainstream labor unions that had long excluded them. AFL president Samuel Gompers viewed Mexicans as a "menace" and a "great evil,"[16] but the Western Federation of Miners (WFM) opened its ranks to everyone and in 1905 helped organize the famed Industrial Workers of the World (IWW), better known as the Wobblies.

Instead of concentrating on one industry, the Wobblies advocated "one big union" to incorporate all workers. They dreamed of a government run by working people, what they called a true "industrial democracy." Unlike the other unions, they welcomed women workers (a fifth of the nation's labor force), workers of all races, the unemployed, and the homeless into their ranks—and elevated some into leadership positions. Activist women like Mary Harris Jones, affectionately called "Mother Jones" by workers she recruited into the United Mine Workers (UMW) union, attended the IWW's founding convention.

Encouraged by the PLM and the Wobblies, Mexicans and Mexican Americans escalated their union-organizing activities. They won several important strikes. By 1911 their California-based Unión de Jornaleros Unidos [United Dayworkers Union] was accepted by the 2-million-strong AFL as an affiliate.

But the virus of racism remained virulent. As the Mexican Revolution of 1910–20 raged on, more Mexicans were crossing the border to flee the warfare. Now in the States in larger numbers, they came under increasing attack. Mexicans were scapegoated for the 1913 economic depression.

A 1913–14 coal-mining strike by Mexican, Greek, Serbian, and Italian members of the UMW in southern Colorado led to the bloody Ludlow Massacre in 1914. The Mexicans originally had been brought in to break Colorado's 1903 coal strikes. Later they joined the union. Daily violence against the miners by goons brought in by the coal companies was widely publicized.

Pressured to do something, the U.S. House of Representatives Committee on Mines and Mining called in East Coast billionaire John D. Rockefeller, Jr., absentee owner of 40 percent of the stocks and bonds of the largest coal company, to answer some questions. Asked about the refusal of company officials to recognize the union, Rockefeller told the congressmen, "We expect to stand by the [company] officers at any cost." The committee chairman then asked Rockefeller: "And you will do that if that costs all your property and kills all your employees?" Replied Rockefeller: "It is a great principle."[17]

He and the other owners stuck by their "great principle."

Evicted from company housing, some 12,000 miners with their wives and children erected tent colonies. On the morning of April 20, 1914, militiamen called in by the owners sprayed the largest settlement with machine-gun fire. At dusk, national guardsmen crept in and set the tents on fire. People rushed out from their flaming tents, some of them with their clothing ablaze. Twenty-six people, including at least eleven Mexicans, perished from suffocation or burns. Eight of the twenty-six were children. Three additional strikers were shot and killed while being held prisoner. Ten days of counterviolence by armed miners ended when President Woodrow Wilson dispatched federal troops. The death toll mounted to sixty-six before the strike ended.[18]

A presidential commission investigated the tragedy and condemned the companies' actions, but it was too late for the dead miners and their families. There is no record of Rockefeller's ever apologizing for the Ludlow Massacre.

The brutality at Ludlow served only to increase the determination of the miners to struggle for a better life. By 1915, miners were able to launch a more successful strike in the Morenci-Clifton area than the 1903 debacle. Once again the central issue was Mexican wages. Thousands of workers from three unions of Mexican miners demanded a $3.50-per-day minimum for *all* underground miners regardless of race. Although one company sealed up the mouth of a mine with cement and told the strikers to "go back to Mexico," and the National Guard was finally sent in to break the nineteen-week strike, the miners won their main demands.[19]

In 1916 the firing of more than 1,000 Mexican miners at Ajo, Arizona, set off a two-year strike wave throughout the mining camps and towns run by Phelps Dodge, Jackling, and Guggenheim. Despite vicious anti-Mexican campaigns, U.S.-born and foreign-born miners banded together to demand the right to organize unions and an end to the racism. That new spirit of solidarity contributed to the growth of the unions. By the spring of 1917, Arizona mine locals had a membership of 5,000 Mexican miners. The nation's labor union movement planned new strikes against the copper companies. Even Gompers's AFL resolved at its state convention to compete with the popular IWW and organize 14,000 Mexican miners in Arizona. However, they never acted on their plan.[20]

World War I was raging in Europe when the United States entered the fray in April 1917. The minerals dug from the earth by the miners were urgently needed by the arms industry. Now the mine owners used the war effort and demands for "patriotism" to attempt to defeat striking miners. That summer in Bisbee, Arizona, Cochise County sheriff Harry Wheeler, who in earlier years had replaced Rynning as captain of the Arizona Rangers, accused striking Mexican copper miners of disloyalty to the war effort and subversion. He and his deputies seized the town's telegraph and telephone office to cut off communications with the outside world. Then, with the aid of the Bisbee Loyalty League, a nativist organization dedicated to ridding the United States of "foreign scum," the lawmen rounded up at gunpoint 1,200 Mexican Americans and Mexicans for deportation.

Mike Foudy, a native-born American of Irish ancestry never forgot what happened: "Men were herded out of their homes . . . into boxcars . . . left in Columbus, New Mexico. They were just dumped in the desert like a bunch of animals. . . . The reason all this happened was that the companies didn't want a union." Slav immigrant Katie Pintek, whose husband was mistakenly thrown on a truck and almost deported, said it was "worse than anything I ever saw in Europe. . . . What it was was that the company was fighting the strike. . . . There were men with guns on porches. They would say that if the company gave them five dollars to kill some son-of-a-bitch, they would. That give me a chill. . . . What kind of America was that?"[21]

President Wilson sent Labor Mediation Commission counsel and future Supreme Court justice Felix Frankfurter to Arizona to report on the Bisbee situation. What Frankfurter found was "a glaring inconsistency between our democratic purposes in this war abroad and the autocratic conduct of some at home."[22]

The president of Phelps Dodge was indicted, but when things quieted down, the charges were dropped. The powerful Eastern investors knew they could still count on government support against the unions.

Wilson had already dispatched 100,000 federalized national guardsmen to help quell the strikes. In the name of patriotism and the war effort, the 1917 Espionage Act and 1918 Sedition Act were used to round up and deport pro-union Latino workers and organizers on the grounds of their alleged lack of patriotism in World War I, despite their loyal participation in the war (see Chapters 4 and 5). War Department directives allowed troops to raid IWW headquarters and patrol freight cars for Mexican migrant activists. For the next few years, U.S. troops conducted an intimidating campaign against labor reformers in the Arizona and Montana copper camps. At Los Angeles' Pacific Sewer Pipe Company, striking Mexicans were accused of "pro-German" subversion. They were also accused of associating with anarchists, a vague term used against the IWW but also used to label anyone struggling for social justice.

In 1918, 101 IWW leaders were tried and convicted on conspiracy charges. They were meted out long sentences and fined the huge sum of $2.5 million. It was a devastating blow for the nation's labor union movement. President Wilson broadened exemptions from immigration restrictions to allow recruiters to bring in large numbers of Mexicans to break strikes, including one in 1919 at the Chicago-Calumet steel complex where Mexican and other workers had unionized.

The 1919–20 Palmer Raids, ordered by the Justice Department's A. Mitchell Palmer, rounded up 10,000 suspected "Reds," many of them Jewish, Italian, Spanish, and Latino activists who were deported back to Europe and the Caribbean or Mexico. The Palmer Raids' brutal violations of due process of law drew frequent but ineffective complaints from Congress and the press. Several states, including California, enacted new laws labeling unions criminal conspiracies.

All these measures, combined with increased deportations at gunpoint of Mexican strikers in the West and Midwest, ended the strike waves and introduced a period of so-called normalcy—the 1920s. With the war over, patriotism could no longer be used to prevent labor activism. Public outrage by middle-class people who sympathized with the plight of working people made companies reluctant to use violence against workers. After Ludlow, even Rockefeller introduced token concessions to labor through a form of "company unionism." To win the eight-hour day and a living wage, however, workers could not rely on favors from the companies. It would take a major depression in the 1930s and a massive organizing campaign.

With millions of new mouths to feed in the United States, agriculture was booming, along with industrialization. Refrigerated railway cars, new canning techniques, and the consolidation of large farms revolutionized food production and increased the demand for cheap labor to cultivate and harvest the crops. The majority of farmworkers were Mexicans, brought into the agricultural fields of California, Texas, and other states.

Long before Cesar Chavez's United Farm Workers gained the nation's attention in the 1960s (see Chapter 6), Mexicans began organizing for the rights of all farmworkers. As early as the 1880s and 1890s, Mexicans, Filipinos, and Japanese launched strikes in California's farm fields. They were not alone in the call for farmworker justice. From 1888 to 1891, the "Colored Alliance" of southern farmworkers mounted what one scholar has called "the most important movement of black Southerners between Reconstruction and the Civil Rights era."[23] Simultaneously, the all-white Farmers Alliance, many of whose members had lost their farms to the banks and big combines, also stood up for rural social justice.

Latino and other immigrant workers were scapegoated for the unemployment caused by the 1907–08 depression. New laws authorized the deportation of aliens who became public charges (paupers). President Teddy Roosevelt barred the entry of Japanese laborers. In unannounced raids on workplaces and Latino residential neighborhoods, lawmen rounded up and deported people.

But farm owners depended on immigrant workers. Few Americans were willing to work in the hot sun for pennies. Conditions were so terrible that many Mexican workers slipped away from the farms and tried to go home. Some growers kept "their" Mexicans handcuffed at night to prevent their escape. When they needed more workers to harvest their crops, they turned to the government for help. In 1909, for example, a U.S.-Mexico treaty guaranteed the importation of 1,000 Mexicans to harvest California's sugarbeet crop. The government further expanded legal importation of Mexican workers in 1917 because of labor shortages caused by World War I. Upon farmers' requests, the government even lifted an unprecedented eight-dollar head tax for entry. Cotton growers' associations imported tens of thousands of Mexicans in the early 1920s. A "revolving door" of importation-deportation of Mexican farmworkers became standard practice—importing them when needed and deporting them when not needed.[24]

Mexican farmworkers found a friend in the IWW. At the peak of Wobbly organizing, Mexicans from the IWW's Agricultural Workers Organization accounted for half of the IWW's total annual dues.[25] After the IWW was broken, Mexican *mutualistas* founded groups championing farmworkers in Colorado, Arizona, Texas, and California. Mexicans and other Latinos were at the forefront of many agricultural strikes until the collapse of the economy in the Great Depression of 1929.

The worldwide Depression—lasting more than ten years, right up to World War II—shook this country to its foundations. By 1932 a quarter of the population had no jobs. Hunger stalked the land. A story about New York City mayor Fiorello La Guardia, the former congressman of "Spanish Harlem" so popular with the city's Puerto Ricans (see Chapter 5), illustrates how tough things were. On a wintry day the mayor used his magistrate powers to attend a police court. He fined an old man ten dollars for stealing a loaf of bread to feed his family. Then the mayor himself paid the fine and told the shocked spectators: "I hereby fine every person in this room fifty cents apiece, except the prisoner, for living in a town where a man has to steal in order to eat."[26]

Among the hardest hit were farmworkers. Employers tried to economize by treating them worse than ever. According to one historian, "Conditions forced Mexicans . . . to become angry strikers. An all-out war erupted in which growers relied on the Immigration Service to deport leaders, pressured state and federal agencies to deny Mexicans relief, used local and state authorities to terrorize workers, killed and imprisoned strikers."[27]

Thousands of Mexican strikers paralyzed cantaloupe

and lettuce production in California's Imperial Valley strikes of 1928 and 1930. A 1933 strike in the strawberry fields of El Monte (Los Angeles County) unified Mexican and Japanese workers and forced the growers to recognize the union. One result was the formation of the statewide 10,000-member Confederation of Mexican Peasants and Workers. California's cotton strikes of 1933–34 and agricultural strikes of 1936 involved tens of thousands more. The situation was similar in other states.[28]

Union organizing and strike waves swept across the nation in those troubled times. Several new tactics were used by industry to hold back people's demands for a decent standard of living and humane work conditions. Since leftists—communists, socialists, and anarchists—supported the struggles of working people and some of the union leaders belonged to radical political parties, all strikers and union leaders were "Red-baited"—called communists and un-American. The new label provided an excuse for hired thugs and National Guard units to beat up and even kill Latinos and other strikers.

When Red-baiting failed, the ultimate card played by employers and their friends in government to restrain labor organizing was an updated "revolving door"—importing Mexicans to undermine union wage scales and deporting the ones who were pro-union. The old racist virus made the job easier. In the early 1930s, with employers and workers alike seeking a scapegoat for the Depression, there occurred a fresh outbreak of anti-Latino hysteria. From coast to coast, authorities rounded up and deported from 400,000 to a million "illegal alien" (and sometimes U.S.-born) Latinos. Many families suffered a human tragedy of unprecedented proportions. Most Latinos, U.S. citizens included, lived in fear.

As soon as one group of Mexican pro-union "troublemakers" was deported, another group of fresh hands was brought in. Employers imported up to a half million Mexican workers during the rest of the 1930s. When the deportees who turned around and reentered the country were added to that number, there were by 1940 an estimated million "illegal Mexicans" living alongside the 1.4 million U.S.-born Mexicans.

The border door still revolves today. The final lyrics of folksinger Woody Guthrie's "Deportee" ballad sums up the fate of many Mexican immigrants: "To fall like dry leaves and rot on the topsoil/And be known by no name except deportee."

Tampa's Ybor City tobacco workers, mostly Cubans, were also labeled Reds, although most had little affection for what they considered to be the fake socialist regime of dictator Joseph Stalin in the Soviet Union. They had steadfastly maintained their sixty-year struggle for social justice by launching major strikes in 1901, 1910, 1920, and 1931.

Puerto Rican, Mexican, and other Latina women in the International Ladies Garment Workers Union (ILGWU) helped spark some of the nation's most important strikes coast to coast in the 1930s. Cannery workers, packers, and pecan and walnut shellers, many of them Latina women, struck in Texas and other states.

Latina woman leaders emerged in the ranks of the United Cannery, Agricultural, Packing, and Allied Workers of America (UCAPAWA). Swelled by the membership of Mexican and Filipino farmworkers' unions, UCAPAWA claimed 125,000 members by 1938, making it the seventh largest union in the gigantic two-year-old Congress of Industrial Organizations (CIO). The building of the CIO turned the tide and was a big step forward for working people toward winning some social justice for all Americans.[29]

Two of the most prominent Latina leaders to emerge in the 1930s and early 1940s were Guatemala-born Luisa Moreno and Mexico-born Josefina Fierro de Bright. They were elected principal leaders of the 6,000-member

Spanish-Speaking People's Congress (1938–42). Moreno, known as the Congress's founder, had worked as a seamstress near New York City's El Barrio. She had helped organize cigar makers in Florida and pecan shellers in Texas. Several Cubans and Puerto Ricans followed her into the new Congress, which concentrated on a wide range of labor and civil rights issues (see Chapter 5).[30]

Latinos were active in most of the major strikes of the 1930s. They were part of the spontaneous protest "sit-ins" launched by automotive and rubber workers in the mid-1930s and of the 1934 San Francisco general strike launched by longshoremen. These and other militant actions forced many concessions from employers and led to the founding of the CIO in 1936 and the International Longshoremen's and Warehousemen's Union (ILWU) in 1937.

Latinos achieved leadership positions in the ILWU and in some of the CIO locals, especially in mining, ore smelting, and steel. Mexican Americans composed three fourths of the pickets at East Chicago's Inland steel plants in 1937 during the famous unionization drive among the "Little Steel" companies. That campaign led to the Memorial Day Massacre by South Chicago's police, who killed ten and wounded more than a hundred by opening fire on a pro-union parade of workers and their families. Mexican Americans from South Chicago's barrios accounted for 15 percent of the peaceful march, including some who headed the parade.[31]

By the late 1930s, pro-union sentiment had swept the nation, leading to the labor reforms of President Franklin D. Roosevelt's New Deal. Legislation outlawed child labor and mandated a minimum wage, the eight-hour day, social security, unemployment insurance, and workmen's compensation benefits.

High above Chase Creek Canyon, open-pit mining superseded the old methods of extracting ore, and by the 1930s the original town of Metcalf was no more. It had been bulldozed. But the area and its mining struggles had not died. In the 1950s and again in the 1980s, new generations of Mexican Americans would be fighting for their rights (see Chapters 5 and 8). But only a few of the nameless ones who had helped begin it all with their shouts of *"Huelga!"* back in the "Old West" lived to see the fruit of their struggles. Those who were still around when the eight-hour day finally became the law of the land in 1938 had reason to be proud of the role they had played.

cuatro

HANDS
ACROSS
THE
BORDERS

*To take our country
they must take our lives*
— Pedro Albizu
Campos

*Our cause will triumph
because it is justice and love.*
— Augusto César
Sandino[1]

On Palm Sunday, March 21, 1937, hundreds of families dressed in their white clean-pressed finery headed down the street toward the cathedral in Ponce, Puerto Rico. They were on their way to a Te Deum mass in honor of their country's independence martyrs. They averted their eyes from patrolling U.S. soldiers who closed in behind them.

Suddenly there was a crackle of gunfire. . . . Screams, bodies falling, mothers with babies in their arms, fathers pulling their children, hats and palm fronds flying through the air, new rounds of gunfire.

The final toll was at least twenty dead, more than a hundred wounded. "Most of the dead," wrote U.S.-appointed investigator Professor Robert J. Hunter, "were little more than children; none were armed; many were shot in the back while seeking refuge."[2]

When word reached New York City's Spanish Harlem, more than 10,000 infuriated Puerto Ricans marched through the streets. They carried placards denouncing the "Ponce Massacre," an atrocity of "Imperialist America."[3]

The reaction was not unusual. Isolated in ghettoes and feeling the sting of racism, Latinos, far longer than most immigrants, continued to identify their country of origin as "home." Home—Mexico, Puerto Rico, Cuba— was also geographically closer for Hispanics in the United States than for Asians and Europeans.

After 1900, Hispanics continued to reach their "hands across the borders" to support freedom fighters against foreign domination—Puerto Rico's Pedro Albizu Campos, Mexico's Ricardo Flores Magón, Nicaragua's Augusto César Sandino— and more. Each of them turned to Hispanic communities in the United States for support.

Now the "enemy" was often perceived to be not Spain but powerful U.S. business interests defended by the U.S. government. Throughout the twentieth century, the U.S. government repeatedly sent in the Marines. This

"Gunboat Diplomacy" guaranteed the success of what became known as "Dollar Diplomacy"—controlling Latin America through economic interests. President Woodrow Wilson stated in 1916: "The masters of the U.S. government are the combined capitalists and manufacturers. . . . We have got to finance the world in some important degree, and those who finance the world must understand it and rule it with their spirits. . . . I am going to teach the South American republics to elect good men."[4]

Early in the twentieth century, American troops were swarming over the Caribbean and Central America. Besides occupying the U.S. possession of Puerto Rico, they stormed the supposedly independent nations of Cuba, the Dominican Republic, Haiti, Nicaragua, Guatemala, Honduras, and Panama, converting them into U.S. military protectorates.

U.S. officials often directed the occupied countries' customs houses and finances. Marine commandant Major General Smedley D. Butler later confessed the reasons for his military missions: "I was a gangster for Wall Street: I helped make Mexico . . . safe for American oil interests in 1914; I helped purify Nicaragua for the international banking house of Brown Brothers in 1909–1912. . . . I helped make Haiti and Cuba a decent place for the National City Bank boys to collect revenue in. . . . I brought light to the Dominican Republic for American sugar interests in 1916."[5]

When the U.S. Marines returned home, they seldom left behind President Wilson's democratically elected "good men." Instead, they trained national guards, police forces, or armies to take their place. Democracy in Latin America would mean that workers might unionize and then strike, opposition parties might speak out against oppression. Under those circumstances, "American sugar interests" and the "National City Bank boys" would not reap the handsome profits they collected in a more controlled, low-wage society. Unsavory dictators like Cuba's Fulgencio Batista, the Dominican Republic's Rafael Trujillo, and Nicaragua's Anastasio Somoza and his sons could guarantee a safe climate for investors by forcefully keeping working people in their place.

But as long as dictators ruled, there were popular uprisings. Latino workers and middle-class professionals residing in the small but growing Hispanic communities in the United States watched the events closely. Each intervention brought new immigrants to their communities— most recently, Cuban, South American, and Central American political refugees (see Chapter 7).

Many Cuban Americans resented the fact that in exchange for U.S. troop withdrawal in 1902 and recognition of Cuba's independence the "grateful" Cubans granted the United States a permanent naval base at Guantánamo. The Platt Amendment to the new Cuban Constitution acknowledged the U.S. right to intervene to secure "the protection of life, property, and individual liberty."

In 1912, African Cubans sparked an uprising that was quashed by the U.S. Marines. Some of the African-Cuban "freedom fighters" eventually made their way to Florida and joined in the labor union struggles of the Florida tobacco workers.

The 1912 and 1917–22 U.S. military occupations of Cuba paved the way for dictator Gerardo Machado who ensured U.S. economic domination of the island. As early as 1914 Cuba was already the sixth largest purchaser of U.S. goods and services. African Cubans and dark-skinned mulattoes—a majority of the population—suffered extreme discrimination. By the 1950s, Cuba was one of Latin America's most racially segregated societies. The best beaches and public facilities were ruled off limits to African Cubans, and racial intermarriage was prohibited.

In 1933 the Cuban people, struggling for democracy, paralyzed the economy with a national strike. Machado fled, but U.S. special ambassador Sumner Welles hand-picked Batista to lead a "sergeants' revolt" against the popular interim government. U.S. warships patrolled Cuba's shores as Batista's troops stormed factories and murdered striking workers. To stem the tide of opposition, Batista canceled the Platt Amendment and adopted a more democratic constitution in 1940. But words and deeds don't always coincide. Batista set up a bloodthirsty dictatorship that lasted until the Cuban Revolution of 1959.

Under Batista's long rule, Cuba became an Americanized paradise for wealthy tourists, where prostitution and drugs flowed freely. U.S. mobsters, including organized crime's Meyer Lansky, made millions controlling Cuba's gambling and flesh-peddling rackets. U.S. government officials backed up Batista's rule behind the scenes. One ambassador to Cuba commented that "sometimes" he was "more important than the President of Cuba."[6]

In Florida, the hysterical anticommunism known as "McCarthyism" that occurred in the post–World War II Cold War silenced the radical, aging tobacco workers. Nonetheless, they and younger middle-class Cuban exiles in Miami and New York attended talks and fund-raisers on behalf of would-be Cuban revolutionaries attempting to bring democracy to their country. The rebels' most popular leader was a large, well-spoken young lawyer nick-named "El Caballo" ("The Horse"). He quoted heavily from Martí and had Martí's talent for uniting people from different groups. His name was Fidel Castro Ruz, but Cubans called him simply Fidel. They celebrated wildly when his ragtag guerrilla army overthrew Batista in 1959.

Puerto Rico, an outright U.S. colony, also was "Americanized." After 1898, U.S. troops never left Puerto Rico. The 1900 Foraker Act mandated school instruction in English and the students' daily pledge of allegiance to the U.S. flag. However, Puerto Ricans defended their own language and culture so strongly that, almost a half century later, these requirements had to be dropped. Administered by the U.S. government, Puerto Rico was not even allowed to elect its own governor until 1947.

Just one month before the United States entered World War I, Congress passed the Jones Act making Puerto Ricans U.S. citizens. Now it became possible to induct 18,000 young Puerto Ricans into the U.S. military. Just as African Americans were assigned to segregated units, Puerto Ricans also were separated from white military personnel.

Puerto Ricans were only halfway American citizens. The Jones Act, most of its provisions still in effect today, did not allow them to vote in U.S. presidential elections. Their representation in the U.S. Congress was limited to a resident commissioner in the House of Representatives, who has a voice but no vote in legislation pertaining to Puerto Rico. To sweeten the bitter pill, Puerto Ricans were exempted from U.S. taxes.

By 1920 up to 20,000 Puerto Ricans had migrated to forty-four states, some having remained after the end of World War I, others purchasing passage or stowing away on ships. Their U.S. citizenship made entering the country easier for them than for other immigrants. Another 40,000 arrived during the 1920s. Most gravitated to New York hoping to find decent jobs. Instead, they were assigned to low-wage jobs most other Americans would not accept. They cleaned out bathrooms and kitchens for restaurants and hotels or labored long hours in unsafe garment "sweatshops." By the 1930s, when the Great Depression crippled the U.S. economy, many Puerto Ricans headed back home to their beloved "Boriquén," where they could remain poor in a warmer climate.

During those years most Puerto Ricans identified with the fight for national independence and economic justice taking place on the island. Some backed the Popular Democratic Party (PPD), founded in 1939 as a pro-independence party. The PPD leader was Luis Muñoz Marín, Puerto Rico's first popularly elected governor. He remained in that post from 1948 until 1964. Shortly after he became governor, he dropped his support for independence.

The most popular leader of all championed the cause of freedom throughout his life. Ponce lawyer and Harvard graduate Pedro Albizu Campos, also known as El Maestro ("The Teacher"), founded the Nationalist Party in 1928 and eventually gained almost mythological status as a symbol of Puerto Ricans' desire for independence. An admirer of José Martí, Albizu Campos hoped to attract Puerto Ricans from all social classes under the banner of "Puerto Rico for the Puerto Ricans."

After losing the 1932 elections, the Nationalist Party dropped out of electoral politics, claiming there never could be fair elections so long as Puerto Ricans had to vote at the "gunpoint" of thousands of U.S. troops occupying the island. In 1936, Albizu Campos was jailed on the charge of advocating the "overthrow of the government of the United States established in Puerto Rico." There followed peaceful protests on both the island and the mainland. In more than half of Puerto Rico's municipalities, Puerto Rican "American citizens" lowered American flags and replaced them with Puerto Rican flags. The protests ended after the bloody Ponce Massacre and the repression of the *independistas* that followed it.

Miraculously, an all Puerto Rican jury acquitted Albizu Campos. The government appealed, and he was subsequently convicted by a jury with only two Puerto Ricans serving on it. He spent the next ten years in Atlanta's federal penitentiary, far from his supporters at home. When he was finally freed, he continued the struggle, refusing to be broken by his persecutors. For the rest of his life he spent only four years outside of prison walls, becoming one of the world's most famous political prisoners. In the Atlanta prison in 1956 a stroke left him partially paralyzed and unable to speak more than two words at a time. His cellmate, Carlos Feliciano, claimed his failing health was brought on by deliberate mistreatment "at the hands of the Americans."[7] Shortly before his death in 1965, Albizu Campos was pardoned by outgoing governor Muñoz Marín.

Albizu Campos's funeral brought out the largest number of mourners in Puerto Rican history. Entire peasant families walked miles to attend. His U.S. defense attorney, African-American human rights activist Conrad Lynn, later recalled him as "very religious . . . the most completely selfless and humble man I had ever met."[8] Latin American countries erected statues in Albizu Campos's honor, as they had done earlier for Martí.

Albizu Campos's jailing and death and the repression of all dissenters as "communists" during the McCarthy era of the late 1940s and the 1950s weakened the Nationalist Party. Special laws, later found to be unconstitutional, were used to jail party members. Because of the initial though short-lived successes of "Operation Bootstrap" in improving the island's standard of living, the Nationalist Party's appeals for economic justice had a diminishing impact.

Introduced in the 1940s, Operation Bootstrap began to industrialize Puerto Rico. Unemployment dropped as 60,000 Puerto Ricans went off to fight World War II and others obtained jobs constructing U.S. military bases in Puerto Rico or working in U.S. war plants. Investors, taking advantage of the tax-free conditions and the low wages in Puerto Rico—one fourth of those paid in the United States—set up hundreds of manufacturing plants that provided 35,000 jobs—mostly to women in light industry.

Shortly after World War II ended and job opportunities decreased, new cheap flights connected the island to the mainland. As part of its antipoverty program, the PPD government organized the outmigration of a third of the population—a million people. Although many were jobless displaced *jíbaros* ("peasants"), half were skilled or semiskilled factory workers. Most became low-wage industrial and service employees in the United States. Some became "commuter" migrants, doing seasonal "stooped labor" in New Jersey and Long Island farm fields. About 20,000 Puerto Rican contract farm laborers still come to the United States every summer.

The Muñoz Marín–PPD administration also decided to cut back population growth. In newly constructed hospitals it encouraged the sterilization of women. By the 1970s more than one third of Puerto Rican women of reproductive age were sterilized.[9]

Starting in 1950 the U.S. Congress began passing additional laws aimed at isolating the *independistas*. With the Nationalist Party on its last legs and the general sentiment for independence slowed down by new hopes for economic justice, Nationalists made two last-ditch efforts to draw attention to their cause. The first was a failed attempt to assassinate President Harry Truman in 1950. The second was a 1954 attack on the U.S. Congress, wounding five congressmen.

Not only were the Nationalists jailed, but racism against Puerto Ricans in the United States went into high gear, with all of "them" viewed as potential terrorists. The independence struggle was not revived until the 1960s, when the Civil Rights Movement emboldened all fighters for social justice. The Nationalist leaders languished in jail until President Jimmy Carter, pressured by an international campaign to free Puerto Rico's "political prisoners" that was sparked by Puerto Rican activists in the United States, pardoned them.

The legislation that had inflamed the Nationalists eventually converted Puerto Rico into today's "commonwealth." A 1952 referendum to approve a commonwealth constitution passed by a four-to-one margin. There was no independence option on the ballot.

If "hands across the border" linkups were strong

among Puerto Ricans and Cubans, they were even tighter among Mexicans. The early 1900s cross-border working-class solidarity added to the already strong ties of Mexican family and friendship networks.

Under Díaz's thirty-five-year dictatorship, Mexico had become a land of extreme contrasts. Poverty and illiteracy plagued a whopping 84 percent of the people. Foreigners—mostly American and British—owned Mexico's abundant oil reserves and about one sixth of its land surface. According to oil millionaire Edward L. Doheny, among others, the first U.S. workers in Mexico "carried arms" and treated Mexicans with "a domineering spirit."[10] When the Mexican Revolution erupted in 1910, some Mexican revolutionaries attacked not just Díaz's soldiers but foreign properties as well.

The Revolution's most skilled organizers were the U.S.-based political exiles who had been active in the great strikes of the Southwest and northern Mexico, the *Magonistas,* members of the PLM led by popular labor organizer and journalist Ricardo Flores Magón.[11] They had issued the party program in St. Louis and led Mexico's "precursor revolts" and strikes of 1906–10 that laid the groundwork for the Revolution. Their program called for human rights and liberal democracy. Later it became a basis for the Mexican Constitution of 1917, still in effect today.[12]

Outlawed in Mexico, the *Magonistas* set up "Liberal clubs" throughout the United States. Their democratic goals and labor organizing attracted many Mexican-American supporters, distressing employers and their friends in government. The *Magonistas* were hounded and threatened, their mail was opened, and they were often thrown into jail on flimsy charges.

Mexican Americans protested when they heard of Flores Magón's jailing in 1907. Solidarity came from all sides, ranging from U.S. socialist presidential candidate Eugene Debs to the far more conservative AFL leader

Santa Fe, New Mexico, is the oldest capital in the United States. Many of today's Hispanic residents are descendants of the first Spanish and Mexican settlers.

TEXAS!!

Emigrants who are desirious of assisting Texas at this important crisis of her affairs may have a free passage and equipments, by applying at the

NEW-YORK and PHILADELPHIA HOTEL,

On the Old Levee, near the Blue Stores.

Now is the time to ensure a fortune in Land: To all who remain in Texas during the War will be allowed 1280 Acres.
To all who remain Six Months, 640 Acres.
To all who remain Three Months, 320 Acres.
And as Colonists, 4600 Acres for a family and 1470 Acres for a Single Man.

New Orleans, April 23d, 1836.

An advertisement offering Americans free transportation, supplies, and land to settle in the Mexican owned territory of Texas.

This picture, entitled The Fandango, *was painted in Texas circa 1848. It is evidence of the continuing Hispanic cultural tradition in Texas.*

Facing page:
The fort of the Alamo, built when Texas was a part of Mexico. The admission of Texas as a state in 1845 resulted in the Mexican-American War and the United States' annexation of half of Mexico's territory.

During the Gold Rush to California in 1849, many Mexican miners were pushed aside as the forty-niners set up their homes on Mexican-American lands. Above is a group of gold miners.

Many Mexican workers built the railroads of the Southwest and led the strikes of railroad workers against the powerful industrialists.

The tent city of a mining camp. In the Ludlow, Colorado, coal miners' strike, national guardsmen set the miners' tents on fire, killing twenty-six Mexicans, eight of them children.

President Woodrow Wilson dispatched 100,000 federalized national guardsmen to put down strikes in the mines of the Southwest. He also interfered in the internal affairs of Latin America, with long-term consequences. Wilson stated in 1916, "The masters of the U.S. government are the combined capitalists and manufacturers . . . Those who finance the world must . . . rule it with their spirits. . . . I am going to teach the South American republics to elect good men."

The Spanish-American War in 1898 lasted ten weeks. African-American troops were the vanguard at the battle of San Juan Hill, Cuba. As a result of the American victory, Cuba was occupied by U.S. troops and Spain ceded Puerto Rico to the United States.

In 1933, United States special ambassador to Cuba Sumner Welles handpicked Colonel Fulgencio Batista (above) to lead an army revolt against the Cuban government. Batista ruled Cuba as a dictator until he was ousted by the Cuban Revolution led by Fidel Castro in 1959.

Hispanic farmworkers have organized in the Southwest for fair labor practices and better living conditions from the late 1800s until today.

Mexican farmworkers and their families in the Southwest endured terrible living and working conditions during the Depression. A Hispanic mother and child were living in this crowded shack on the side of the fields.

Pedro Albizu Campos (second from right), leader of the Puerto Rican Nationalist Party, is arrested at his home in San Juan, Puerto Rico, following an attempt by extreme nationalists to assassinate President Harry Truman on November 2, 1950. Campos, a lawyer and a Harvard University graduate, advocated independence for Puerto Rico.

Mexicans accused of illegally crossing the United States–Mexico border in 1953 are taken off a freight train in which they had been hiding. This was part of the U.S. government's "Operation Wetback."

Cesar Chavez (front left), president of the United Farm Workers union (UFW), and Walter Reuther (front, holding sign), president of the United Auto Workers union (UAW), lead a picket line in California in 1965. The picketers were seeking to have the UFW recognized as a union. The Spanish word huelga *on the signs means "strike."*

A Quaker group gave sanctuary to this father and two daughters from El Salvador. They must conceal their identities with masks while testifying about atrocities committed by the Salvadoran army.

On the last day to file for amnesty, May 4, 1988, people who have entered the United States without proper documents stand on line at the Immigration and Naturalization Service office in Los Angeles to apply for amnesty and obtain naturalization papers.

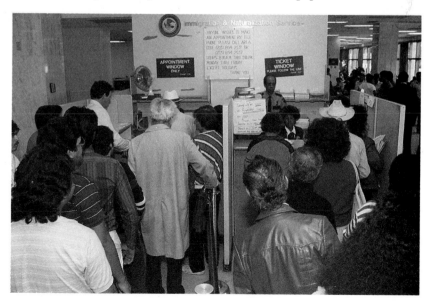

Seeking political asylum in the United States, this three-year-old Guatemalan boy and his mother and sister (background) wait patiently in a Red Cross shelter in Brownsville, Texas. Many Central American refugees seek asylum from political persecution and civil war in their countries.

Samuel Gompers. Especially active in efforts to gain the release of "Mexican political prisoners" was the popular seventy-eight-year-old Mother Jones.[13]

Finally released in 1910, Flores Magón helped coordinate the Mexican Revolution's first uprisings. By early 1911 the *Magonistas* had waged armed struggles in Mexico, winning control of Mexicali and much of Baja California. In Baja they set up anarchist-style communal areas, cooperative democracies governed from below. Wobblies from the IWW, some of them Mexican-American, fought alongside the *Magonistas* in Baja, proving their call for international solidarity in deeds rather than just words.[14] This rarely seen solidarity was used by PLM opponents to accuse party members of being "Yankee agents." After dictator Díaz's defeat by PLM and other armed rebels in May 1911, Mexico's democrats fought among themselves and the PLM lost control of Baja.

Flores Magón and the PLM were very popular in the Mexican-American barrios of the Southwest. In mid-1911 Flores Magón, his brother, and other PLM leaders were again arrested. Mexican Americans from the Los Angeles barrio jammed the courtroom. Their heroes were convicted and spent the next several years in and out of U.S. jails. With them incarcerated, new popular leaders emerged inside Mexico, hardworking men like Francisco "Pancho" Villa in the north and Emiliano Zapata in the south.[15]

With dictator Díaz gone, wealthy industrialist Francisco I. Madero was elected as the Revolution's first president. But the Army and the American ambassador objected to Madero's slowness in disarming the still-active revolutionaries. In 1913 some disgruntled pro-Díaz generals met in the U.S. Embassy (the "Pact of the Embassy") to engineer a military coup and Madero's assassination. The coup caused Mexico to erupt in full-scale revolution.

President-elect Wilson was appalled. Once he took office, he launched a successful campaign to rid Mexico of the coup leaders who had sided with British oil interests. He dispatched U.S. troops to occupy Veracruz, where one of the Revolution's warring factions, led by a crusty upper-class former state governor, Venustiano Carranza, set up a rump government. Wilson eventually backed Carranza against Villa and Zapata.

Hypocritically denouncing the "Yankee intervention," Carranza was more than happy to be propped up by U.S. diplomatic recognition, loans, and arms. In 1915, U.S. authorities, usually distrustful of labor unions, looked the other way while Carranza supporters in Los Angeles organized the Constitutionalist Union of Mexican Workers. When the U.S. government blocked arms shipments to Carranza's rivals, Villa felt betrayed. After all, his troops had protected the vast Mexican landholdings of journalist William Randolph Hearst and other U.S. millionaires in exchange for noninterference in the "hands across the border" smuggling of ammunition.

In 1916 an angry Villa launched a hit-and-run raid on Columbus, New Mexico. Villa's attack added fuel to the flames of anti-Mexican hysteria then sweeping the country. Racists and mine owners used it to justify their brutal assaults on striking miners. The United States invaded northern Mexico with 6,000 troops led by General John J. Pershing. To the south, Carranza's U.S.-backed forces quickly gained the military upper hand against Villa, who was giving Pershing a not-so-merry chase. Pershing withdrew his troops in January 1917. By then Carranza's victory was assured.

After the Mexican Revolution, hungry and persecuted Mexicans and other Latin Americans continued to seek refuge and jobs in the United States. But most Central Americans could not afford the long trip to the United States and stopped in Mexico or Costa Rica. One of them worked for a U.S. oil company in Tampico, on Mexico's

Gulf coast. His name was Augusto César Sandino. Nicaragua's Sandinista revolution of 1979 was named after him.

In 1924, Sandino saw U.S. gunships pull into Tampico, Mexico, to guarantee the interests of Standard Oil. Condemning "Yankee imperialism," he returned to Nicaragua, purchased some guns, and found twenty-nine miners willing to join him. For almost a decade some 4,000 marines waged a losing war against Sandino's guerrilla army. In 1927, U.S. planes, searching for Sandino's guerrilas, bombed and machine-gunned fleeing unarmed civilians in Ocotal, leaving 300 dead. U.S. forces not only bombed towns. They shot and tortured prisoners, mutilated opponents' bodies, and created a "concentration camp program" of civilian "relocation camps." Appalled at what they had been called upon to do, some marines deserted and joined Sandino's Defensive Army of National Sovereignty.[16]

Back in the United States, shocked Americans, including Latinos, took to the streets to protest the "immoral, unjust, imperialist war." Responding to popular demands of "Hands Off Nicaragua!" Congress cut off funds for the war. By January 1, 1933, when the United States gave up the fight, Sandino's army numbered 3,000 guerrillas—six times the number of Sandinista guerrillas that later took power in Nicaragua in 1979!

Sandino agreed to a peace pact. The U.S.-trained National Guard was turned over to General Anastasio Somoza, an opponent of Sandino. In short order, Somoza ordered his officers to detain Sandino. In a gangland-style execution, Sandino was mowed down by machine-gun fire. Somoza assured the executioners that the U.S. ambassador had told him the U.S. government recommended Sandino's elimination. During the next five years, some 20,000 peasants, workers, and students fell before a hail of Guard bullets. Latin America's longest-lasting family tyranny had begun: the forty-five-year Somoza dynasty.

In response to criticism of U.S. support for Somoza, President Franklin D. Roosevelt said: "Somoza is an S.O.B., but he is *our* S.O.B."[17]

The trip to the United States from Nicaragua was expensive. Those who could afford it fled Somoza's dictatorship and lent support to courageous fighters for democracy back home.

Events in Guatemala paralleled Nicaragua's story. When Guatemalans overthrew the fourteen-year-long dictatorship of Jorge Ubico in 1944, they conducted democratic elections. In 1954, Jácobo Arbenz was the nation's president. During his election campaign he had promised to carry out a land reform. At the time, the Boston-based United Fruit Company and other foreign concerns owned 98 percent of Guatemala's cultivated land. In a cautious program, Arbenz intended to distribute United Fruit's unused lands to landless peasants and reimburse the company. United Fruit directors cried "Communism!" and telephoned their friends in high places.

The CIA's "Operation Success" swung into high gear. It set up training camps in Honduras and Nicaragua for a special mercenary force to invade Guatemala. In 1954, U.S. planes bombed Guatemala City and other government strongholds into submission. The leader of the mercenaries set up a puppet government loyal to the United Fruit Company and ordered opponents to be jailed or shot. U.S. military aid and training missions poured in to defend the new regime against the real believers in democracy.

By 1985 the grisly statistics of thirty years of Guatemala's state terrorism told all: 100,000 dead, 50,000 disappeared (and presumed dead), and a million refugees.[18] Among the people fleeing were many Indians and poor people. Those who managed to make the long trek overland across Mexico sneaked across the U.S. border and mixed in with throngs of Mexican migrant workers. In the United States, Latinos and others launched a campaign to grant them political refugee status (see Chapter 7).

While many Hispanics closely followed the events back home, they also became increasingly involved in the struggle for civil rights here. In the urban barrios and the distant farm fields from New York to California, the cry for freedom and equality was about to ring out.

EARLY

CIVIL RIGHTS

STRUGGLES

*Respect your citizenship
and preserve it;
honor your country,
maintain its tradition
in the spirit of its citizens,
and embody your self into its
culture and civilization.*
                    — The LULAC Code, 1929

*The Mexican People in their
struggles for first-class citizenship
are becoming more and more
aware that the only way to win
this fight is to have the closest unity
with our strongest ally,
the Negro people.*
                    — Virginia Ruiz, officer of the
                        Asociación Nacional
                        México-Americana
                        (ANMA), 1951[1]

It was early 1929, not long before the devastating economic collapse known as the Great Depression. Twenty-five neatly dressed men sat facing an audience of over a hundred similar men in the Obreros ("Workers") Hall in Corpus Christi, Texas. Most of them were Mexican-American business people and professionals representing organizations like the Sons of America, the Knights of America, and the League of Latin American Citizens. After a long and animated discussion period, they resolved unanimously to hold a constitutional convention for their new organization: LULAC, League of United Latin American Citizens. Little did they realize they were launching the nation's largest, most enduring Hispanic civil rights organization.

Even these more financially successful Hispanics had found that racism blocked their upward climb to success. Central to their purposes at their founding convention was a desire to "prove" their "American-ness." To further this goal, they restricted LULAC membership to American *citizens* of Latin extraction.

LULAC members embraced the melting pot idea. To "melt," or assimilate into the dominant culture, of course, meant you had to be "white," or at least act as if you were. In keeping with this attitude, and to escape the legalized segregation of African Americans in states like Texas, LULAC's founders referred to Mexican Americans as "the first white race to inhabit this vast empire of ours."[2] Adopting English as its official language, LULAC called for developing "the best, purest and most perfect type of a true and loyal citizen of the United States of America."[3] Since the U.S. Constitution and Bill of Rights guaranteed equality, LULAC intended to go through the courts to fight bigotry.

The setting for the founding of civil rights organizations like LULAC was the 1920s era of resurgent nativism. During an economic recession in 1921, politicians and journalists accused darker-skinned peoples who spoke with "foreign accents" of "taking American jobs." The 1924 Immigration Act established a quota system that slammed the door on most nonwhite immigrants, guaranteeing the predominance in the United States of white people from northern Europe.

It was the heyday of the eugenics movement. White educators talked of "criminal genes" and "biological housecleaning." Half the states passed sterilization laws applicable to "inferior" people variously defined. Future Nazis in Germany studied U.S. eugenics "science," later to apply their own genocidal forms of "race cleansing" against six million Jews. Magazines published pseudoscientific articles labeling Mexicans and other Latinos a "eugenic menace." Chicago congressman Martin Madden called Mexicans "the worst element." Widely read author T. Lothrop Stoddard asserted Mexicans were "inferior" and "born communist."[4]

Many officials who witnessed murders of Mexicans did nothing. In 1922 a liquored-up mob hauled a randomly selected "greaser" prisoner out of a jail in Weslaco, Texas, and strung him up to the nearest lamppost as jeering spectators and jail guards looked on. Commented *The New York Times*: "The killings of Mexicans [in Texas] without provocation is so common as to pass almost unnoticed."[5] Acts of police brutality against anyone who "looked Mexican" became commonplace. A Latino community newspaper in Chicago complained in 1926: "We are being made the victims of the police in Chicago and other cities."[6]

In the border areas between Mexico and the United States, Mexican and Central American immigrants faced a new kind of "welcoming committee." In 1924 the nation's first and only national police force was created, the U.S. Border Patrol. Many of the new employees of the Border Patrol and the Immigration and Naturalization Service, what Latinos came to call *"la migra,"* were outspoken racists.

Abuses and murders became a frequent scenario at the border. Mexican-American defenders of the immigrant workers' human rights appealed to Mexican consulates for help. They cited the Mexican Constitution's Article 123, incorporating the 1906 PLM program's *guarantees* of the rights of Mexicans working outside the country. Mexico's diplomatic corps hesitated to intervene. Consular officials spent most of their time officiating at cultural events like the celebration of Mexican national holidays in the barrios. They didn't want to rock the boat.

By the 1930s and 1940s the majority of the nation's Latinos, including some two million Mexicans, were U.S. citizens. Though small in number, Latino middle-class professionals and merchants knew their constitutional rights and organized to defend them through organizations like LULAC. In a society that ridiculed them as "inferior," "colored," "spics," "greasers," or "niggers" and that placed their children in second-class segregated schools, LULAC members fought for the elusive "American dream" of equal opportunity.

LULAC claimed to be nonpolitical, but it often tied its fortunes to the Democratic Party. In the name of retaining its "nonpolitical" and middle-class character, LULAC opposed the pecan shellers' strike and other union-organized strikes of the 1930s. Despite LULAC's lack of support for their strikes, the "Tex-Mex" workers were so well organized that they were able to elect their own candidate to Congress in 1938.

LULAC stuck to its goal of using the court system to try to achieve racial integration. Over the years, it pressed legal suits for equality in education, public facilities, suffrage, housing, and an end to discrimination in jury selection and to the Deep South's poll tax on nonwhites trying to vote. It also sponsored some police brutality suits. LULAC rarely won court cases involving the police, but it did win occasional victories against owners of restaurants, movie theaters, swimming pools, and other public accommodations that excluded or segregated Latinos.

Often LULAC followed the lead of community activists. Barrio residents everywhere were spending year after year struggling to end segregation, especially in the schools. As early as 1931 parents of seventy-five mostly Mexican-American children in the rural community of Lemon Grove outside San Diego achieved the nation's first successful court challenge to school segregation.[7]

LULAC gained a name for itself as an organization fighting for equality. Within its own ranks, however, women were barred from membership. The more prominent National Association for the Advancement of Colored People (NAACP), founded in 1910, welcomed women and people of all races into membership. In 1934, LULAC reluctantly introduced "Ladies' Councils" to accommodate women wishing to participate.

The Great Depression hit Hispanics, African Americans, and Native Americans especially hard. Latinos were laid off from their jobs, evicted from their homes, hassled by the police, scapegoated for the nation's troubles. An article in a prominent magazine headlined, "Welcome Paupers and Crime: Puerto Rico's Shocking Gift to the U.S."[8] Angry Puerto Ricans in New York City's East Harlem, "El Barrio," marched to protest such slurs and to demand jobs, housing, and food. They often joined with African Americans, Jews, and other oppressed groups to achieve some semblance of social justice. They all backed Vito Marcantonio, East Harlem's congressman from 1934 to 1936 and 1938 to 1950.

Nicknamed "Puerto Rico's congressman," Marcantonio supported Puerto Rican independence and became co-counsel for its jailed spokesperson Albizu Campos. In 1936, he helped found the American Labor Party (ALP). The ALP accounted for the majority of the votes that elected the country's first Puerto Rican officeholder, Oscar García Rivera, who won a state assembly seat in 1937.

When the United States entered World War II, job openings in war production plants took much of the sting out of the Depression. Despite a shortage of workers, however, Latinos and African Americans were the last to be hired for defense jobs. Unemployment persisted in the barrios.

The Spanish-Speaking People's Congress, described in Chapter 3, formed a wartime alliance with the Jewish People's Committee and the NAACP to create the Council for the Protection of Minority Rights. It made only a slight dent in discriminatory hiring practices, although it did persuade the government to create job training programs in Belvedere, California. It embraced the patriotic slogan "Americans All" and strongly opposed the racist states of fascist Italy, Nazi Germany, and Imperial Japan. Hispanic soldiers performed outstandingly in the war, receiving more Medals of Honor than any other group.[9]

Another kind of racial problem surfaced in the war years. After Japan bombed Pearl Harbor, the government ordered the incarceration of the nation's 100,000 Japanese Americans. Nothing comparable was done against German Americans, even though some backed Hitler. They were, after all, white! But it wasn't only the Japanese who suffered. Latinos and African Americans too young to be drafted into the armed services also experienced racist attacks.

One of the most famous incidents occurred in Los Angeles. After a guest leaving a party was found dead in 1942, the police arrested and beat up two dozen members of the "38th Street Club," one of several new "gangs" being organized by Mexican-American youngsters. In an atmosphere of mass anti-Mexican hysteria whipped up by the press, the youths were tried on second-degree murder charges. Nine were convicted and imprisoned. The Spanish-Speaking People's Congress's Josefina Fierro de Bright and others formed the Sleepy Lagoon Defense Committee to help defend the accused, but committee members were spied on by the FBI and branded as un-American. Later, an appeals court reversed the youths' conviction for lack of evidence.

The worst was yet to come. In 1943 sailors and marines in Oakland, California, invaded the Mexican-American and African-American ghetto and beat up on "greasers and niggers." They "de-pantsed" zoot-suiters, as those who wore distinctive peg pants and long jackets were called. The attacks spread to southern California until, by June, sailors were assaulting Hispanics, Filipinos, and African Americans in full-scale riots. Mobs of servicemen and civilians swept through the East Los Angeles barrio shouting "Let's get the chili-eating bastards!" According to statements by officers and enlisted men at the time, the U.S. military encouraged or condoned the attacks. But the press blamed the brawling on "zoot suit hoodlums." A state government investigation later placed the blame where it belonged: on the military and the police. The first commercial Mexican-American movie, the 1981 musical *Zoot Suit*, was based on some of these events.[10]

Hispanic and African-American soldiers returned from World War II with an eye to winning at home what they had defended abroad: democratic rights. Overseas they had experienced a degree of respect and equal treatment denied them in white America. Their outspoken opposition to racism was a critical factor in the development of the broad-based Civil Rights Movement of the late 1950s and early 1960s. The successful anticolonial revolutions of the peoples of Africa and Asia to create independent nations also made an impact on the U.S. government. America's unchanging racism was a handicap to becoming a major leader of the postwar world. President Truman's executive order ending racial segregation in the Armed Forces and the 1954 *Brown* decision banning public school segregation sought to alleviate the international embarrassment.[11]

There were other difficult problems to face, too. If

all of the war plants were closed, joblessness would again plague America. Some believe that it was necessary to create a new "enemy" after the defeat of Germany and Japan in order to keep industry perking. The Cold War against communism became the handiest solution. The communist Soviet Union, the nation's ally in the war, was assigned the role of enemy, even though its factories were bombed out and according to diplomats such as George Kennan it posed no serious military threat. Politicians and employers unleashed an anticommunist witch-hunt known as McCarthyism that curtailed free speech and generated the firings of many social-justice activists. Organized labor's best leaders were purged in the name of fighting communism, which left most unions weakened and thus poor defenders of workers' rights.[12]

During this long period of Red-baiting, LULAC, always careful to avoid actions that would make it appear militant or radical, continued its search for social justice through the courts. In 1946–47 it joined together with the NAACP and other groups to argue a landmark school desegregation case in southern California's Westminster school district that became an important precedent for the more famous *Brown* decision of 1954.[13]

A jury-selection suit argued by LULAC lawyer Gus García dragged through the courts until that same landmark year, 1954. A radical, García was often criticized by more moderate LULAC members. He pointed out that discrimination in jury selection was a violation of the Fourteenth Amendment to the U.S. Constitution. The Supreme Court agreed. Noting that for twenty-five years in Texas not a single Mexican American had ever been selected for jury duty, it ruled that Mexican Americans had been unconstitutionally treated "as a class apart."[14]

Even after their few court victories, Latinos experienced the same old segregation and acts of bigotry. Bolder civil rights groups developed and, tired of LULAC's strictly legalistic approach, became the forerunners of the Latino empowerment movements of the 1960s. Three stood out: the American GI Forum, the Community Service Organization (CSO), and the Asociación Nacional México-Americana (ANMA—National Mexico-American Association).

The GI Forum was founded by Dr. Hector Garcia and World War II veterans when some Texas cemeteries refused to handle the body of a Mexican-American soldier. It lobbyied for more Hispanic political appointments and called for equal benefits for all veterans, desegregation, and an end to police brutality. GI Forum remains active today in more than twenty states.

The CSO used the nonviolent tactics—mass action, bloc voting, and street protests—that Dr. Martin Luther King, Jr., would advocate during the 1960s. It helped organize southern California's Civic Unity Leagues that ran Mexican American candidates for public office—a rare event. The Leagues welcomed women, who played leading roles in voter registration drives. By appealing to the growing number of Mexican American voters, they elected Edward R. Roybal to the Los Angeles City Council in 1949, the first person of Mexican descent to serve since 1881. Future farmworker-union organizer Cesar Chavez became the CSO's general director before leaving the organization in 1962 because of its refusal to back a farm-labor organizing program (see Chapter 6).

In Chicago's older barrios of Mexican American steel and stockyard workers, CSO-style organizations like the Chicago Area Project (CAP) took shape. In Detroit, where 5,000 Mexican Americans made up half the workforce at Great Lakes Steel, Hispanics fought for equal access to jobs, housing, and services through the Latin-American Steelworkers' Club.[15]

ANMA was founded in northern New Mexico after miners clashed with police in 1949. It was promptly labeled communist, infiltrated by the FBI, and hounded out of business by 1955. But in its short life it set important precedents for building unity among workers of different races and for incorporating women on an equal basis into the struggle for social justice.

ANMA's key organizational strength came from leaders of the International Union of Mine, Mill and Smelter Workers (known as Mine-Mill), founded by relatives and friends of the miners who had led the Metcalf-Morenci strikes earlier in the century. Nicaraguan Humberto Silex helped revitalize Mine-Mill in the 1930s and bring it into the CIO. By the 1950s three quarters of copper production workers in the Southwest were Mine-Mill members. In line with the witch-hunt atmosphere of the time, the CIO expelled Mine-Mill in 1950 on the charge of being communist-dominated.

Despite the attack on its leaders, members remained loyal to the union. Mine-Mill led the now famous fifteen-month strike against Empire Zinc in New Mexico. The militant role of Hispanic women pickets was a central theme of the Hollywood blacklisted film, *Salt of the Earth,* that dramatized the strike. The women spent months in jail, but the miners won some of their demands.

Of all of the civil rights organizations, ANMA was the only one to steadfastly oppose the government actions of the Cold War and McCarthyism. It helped circulate the Stockholm Peace Appeal to end the Cold War. ANMA was especially courageous in exposing the violations of civil liberties by the government in deporting people suspected of communist sympathies under the McCarran-Walter Act. President Truman had vetoed the Act as unconstitutional, but Congress overrode the veto.

Organizations like LULAC and the NAACP, on the other hand, did little to defend the right to free speech of suspected "subversives." Instead, LULAC began moving cautiously into the electoral arena. It backed conservative Mexican American air force veteran Raymond Telles, elected mayor of El Paso in 1957.[16]

Other civil rights organizations did not fare as well as LULAC. Members of the Spanish-Speaking People's

Congress were constantly Red-baited. Luisa Moreno was deported. Fierro de Bright fled the United States rather than testify before the House Un-American Activities Committee and supply it with the names of her friends. The congressional inquisitors claimed her colleagues were "guilty by association" with "known communists."[17]

The repressive atmosphere of the Cold War had a big impact on the Puerto Rican community of East Harlem in New York City, too. Marcantonio was accused of being a communist or a fellow traveler. His reelections depended on getting out the Barrio vote. By 1950 there were 63,000 Puerto Ricans in his district. One way to stop Marcantonio's regular electoral victories was to eliminate his supporters from the voting booths. In order to register to vote, Barrio voters had to pass English literacy tests based on white middle-class standards, a discriminatory practice later outlawed by the 1965 Federal Voting Rights Act. White volunteers, many of them Jewish, helped Puerto Ricans prepare for the tests and register to vote.

Marcantonio finally lost an election because of another maneuver in 1950. His district was redrawn to include the conservative "silk stocking" electorate of Manhattan's ritzy Upper East Side. Despite all the ploys against him, he still received 66 percent of El Barrio's vote. Two New York Puerto Ricans later recalled: "People said he was a communist, may the Lord rest his soul, but he was the best New York ever had."[18]

Political participation by most Puerto Ricans ended with Marcantonio's 1950 defeat and the "Red scare." The Democratic Party was moving in a conservative direction and focusing its efforts on recruiting whites of European descent. In 1952, to help get out the vote, a few "politicos" founded a near equivalent to LULAC or NAACP, the Council of Puerto Rican and Spanish Organizations of Greater New York.

Meanwhile, a new outrage against Mexicans occurred. After the Korean War of 1950–53 had pulled America out of an economic slump, the veterans returned to their old jobs. But with no more war to keep armaments plants producing at full capacity, a new recession developed. Mexicans were once again scapegoated for a failing economy and the loss of jobs. In the government's "Operation Wetback," some 1.5 million Mexicans were rounded up and placed in jails or deported across the border. The humiliating term *wetback*—originally used to describe illegal Mexican immigrants who entered the United States by crossing the treacherous waters of the Rio Grande[19]—was applied, then, as it is today, to almost all Mexicans and Central Americans.

Some of Operation Wetback's deportees were U.S. citizens, naturalized Latinos caught in the nationwide dragnet. Other deportees were Mexicans legally in the United States under a 1942 treaty with Mexico known as the Bracero Program (in Spanish, *bracero*—from *brazo,* or "arm"—means "working hand"). The treaty had authorized the use of contract labor (outlawed in 1886) to make up for a labor shortage caused by fourteen million U.S. workers' going off to fight World War II. After the war, the Bracero Program had been extended and the braceros helped create today's highly profitable "agribusiness." Up to half a million braceros were entering the country each year. Through its "supplemental agreements," the 1942 treaty supposedly protected their rights, but they were treated like dirt and maligned as un-American. The U.S. Labor Department executive who oversaw the Bracero Program from 1959 until its demise in 1964 later described it as "legalized slavery."[20]

Operation Wetback coincided with the CIA's 1954 overthrow of Guatemala's supposedly communist government (see Chapter 4) and Senator Joseph McCarthy's televised congressional hearings against generals in the U.S. Army. Much public attention was turned toward those dramatic events, and so efforts by ANMA and other groups to defend the victimized deportees gained little public notice. Senator McCarthy's witch-hunt went too far in its abuse of the generals, and he was later censured by his colleagues for overstepping the bounds in the ongoing campaign against dissent of any kind.[21]

As McCarthyism simmered down in the late 1950s, new Hispanic civil rights groups emerged. Two Puerto Rican-based ones were the educational organizations Aspira and the Puerto Rican Forum. They were harbingers of more intense organizing activities to follow (see Chapter 6).

Life in the barrios was changing rapidly in the 1950s, but rarely for the better. By the 1960s more than 80 percent of all Latinos resided in run-down urban ghettoes. Predominantly white suburbs had sprung up near the major cities. Superhighways were built to link the suburbs to downtown business areas. Urban "renewal" programs resembled urban "removal" of Latinos and African Americans, as either the highways or new high-rent apartment houses were built where their homes once stood.

The Catholic Church's white hierarchy, rarely concerned about the civil rights of its Latino flock, began looking for new parishioners in the big cities that were being abandoned by European Americans. Although the Church turned its attention on them, it continued to discourage Latinos from taking any action for social justice.[22] The Catholic hierarchy in San Antonio from 1940 to 1970 was an exception. In San Antonio the bishops were prounion.

Many young Latinos began to believe that the goslow, legalistic methods of the middle-class assimilationist reformers were not working. A new generation of angry Latinos and African Americans was emerging in poor neighborhoods. The decade of the "silent fifties" was about to give way to "the explosive sixties."

6 *seis*

THE SIXTIES AND SEVENTIES—LATINO EMPOWERMENT

Man! How many times have I stood on the
rooftop of my broken-down building at night
and watched the bulb-lit world below.
Like somehow it's different at night, my Harlem.
There ain't no bright sunlight to reveal the
stark naked truth of garbage-lepered streets.
. . . and I begin to listen to the sounds inside me.
Get angry, get hating angry, and you won't be
scared.

— Piri Thomas, 1967

I am Joaquín
in a country that has wiped out
all my history,
stifled all my pride. . . .

Here I stand
Poor in money
Arrogant with pride.

— Rodolfo "Corky" Gonzales, 1972[1]

One hot summer day in Chicago's black ghetto, older people "taking the air" on their front stoops looked up in surprise. Marching down their street came phalanxes of young people waving Puerto Rican flags, Black Panther flags, and—look again—yes, white folks carrying Confederate flags!

They were chanting "Power to the People!"

One old-timer shook his head and chuckled: "Look at that! Just what do ya suppose those crazy kids are up to *now?*"[2]

After the "silent fifties," the 1960s exploded with that kind of surprise. Far from being a period dominated by "chaos," "hippies," or "druggies," as it is sometimes portrayed, the sixties (and the early seventies) were a time of great conflict when people organized—independently of the Democratic and Republican parties—the largest civil rights, peace, and antipoverty marches in American history. They achieved impressive gains for human dignity and equality.[3]

With 1961's Freedom Rides to integrate public transportation, the six-year-old Civil Rights Movement in the Deep South took a quantum leap, drawing into its orbit northern students, black, white, and Latino. A few years later, the Vietnam War, the longest in the nation's history, triggered the powerful Anti-War Movement. By 1968 it had led to President Lyndon Johnson's decision not to run for a second term in the face of the escalating protests.

Young people from the nation's high schools, colleges, and ghettos organized radical actions demanding a better world. Many were Latinos. The slogans and banners of the 1960s' new activists, including the shouts of "black power" first heard in Mississippi's 1966 civil rights marches, raised the issue of *economic* democracy. To obtain a decent education or job, it was necessary to have some economic clout. The idea of group empowerment became contagious. Latinos, Native Americans, women, gays, even senior citizens (the "Gray Panthers") founded their own empowerment movements.

In the cities, people began to organize to take back control of their own neighborhoods. A Puerto Rican street saying typified the attitude of the day: *"Despierta Borriqua—defiende lo tuyo"* ("Wake up, Puerto Rican—defend what's yours").

A new generation of Latinos asserted leadership in open defiance of LULAC-style reformist strategies. Shouting *"Viva la causa!"* ("Long live the cause [of social justice]!"), farmworkers, students, barrio gang members, prisoners and ex-prisoners, and Vietnam War veterans all swung into action for social justice. They substituted direct mass action for the all-too-often ineffective legal battles of the past. Some of the older reformers came to agree with them and joined them.

The 1964 and 1968 Civil Rights Acts, the 1964 Economic Opportunity Act, the 1965 Voting Rights Act, the 1968 Fair Housing Act, and President Johnson's War on Poverty programs were major historic concessions to the growing movements. These victories convinced many people that the best way to bring about change was through mass action. Politicians listened when people came out into the streets.

Other movements took courage. In 1964 a young Mexican-American woman stood up before a huge throng of students who had been denied the right to set up pro-civil rights literature tables at the University of California-Berkeley campus. She told them to "muster up as much love as you can." Then, strumming her guitar and singing with them the civil rights song "We Shall Overcome," she led them up the steps of the university's administration building. Inside, they set up their literature tables and "freedom classes."

The woman was Joan Baez, the famous folksinger. After Baez left the building, the police arrived and dragged the students down stairwells and off to jail. Berkeley's Free

Speech Movement had come of age. It joined the Civil Rights Movement as the parent of a nationwide student movement for social justice and an end to the Vietnam War.[4]

In 1962 the nation's most exploited labor group, farmworkers—mostly Latinos—gathered in Fresno, California, for the first convention of a new union that later became known as the United Farm Workers (UFW). They chose Mexican Americans Cesar Chavez and Dolores Huerta as their spokespersons. The mother of several children, Huerta was a skilled organizer and speaker. Chavez was a Navy veteran who had grown up picking crops in the fields. He became the first Hispanic to gain national prominence. Like Martin Luther King, he advocated nonviolence. To protest the murders, beatings, and jailings of pro-union farmworkers, he engaged in lengthy fasts.[5]

Chavez later acknowledged that the farmworkers might have never gained public attention if he had not gone to the Berkeley campus in 1965 and asked for help in their strike against grape growers in the Delano, California, area, where half the world's table grapes are grown. The students visited supermarkets and liquor stores, threatening them with a boycott if they didn't stop selling nonunion grapes and the beverages made from them. In 1966 the strikers won an historic first union contract with one of the growers, the Schenley Corporation. But Gallo Wine Company and others held out against the strike.

A turning point in the UFW strike was a hot, grueling 250-mile march from Delano to Sacramento in 1966 (and a similar march in Texas in support of the Rio Grande Valley "great melon strike" of 1966–67). Television cameras rolled as exhausted men, women, and children made their way down hot, dusty roads and told newscasters about the subhuman living conditions of farmworkers. Only the heartless continued to buy grapes.

The Berkeley students' action in California was imitated by activists all over the nation. The U.S. Defense Department assisted the desperate growers by buying grapes and shipping them to the soldiers in Vietnam. But from coast to coast busy weekend shoppers at boycotted supermarkets and liquor stores soon recognized what the words *Viva la huelga!* meant—"Long live the strike!"

By 1969 seventeen million adult Americans refused to buy a single bunch of grapes. Within a year all the grape growers settled with the UFW. To keep up the momentum, the UFW launched a lettuce boycott to help win another hard-fought strike. In 1975 the first legislation recognizing the rights of farmworkers was passed, California's Agricultural Labor Relations Act.

The farmworkers' movement inspired many Mexican Americans who had tried to end discrimination through political party involvement. They had helped to elect John F. Kennedy and backed President Johnson's War on Poverty. But Johnson failed to include them in preplanning sessions for the 1968 White House Conference on Civil Rights. At a 1966 federal jobs conference in New Mexico, Corky Gonzales, the son of migrant farmworkers and an amateur boxing champion, led a Mexican-American walkout in order to protest the president's blindness to the nation's "invisible minority."

For the first time, an American president publicly discussed the issue of civil rights of Hispanics. "President Pledges Aid to Mexican Americans," headlined the *Los Angeles Times*.[6] Despite Johnson's pledge, Gonzales was punished for leading the walkout. Fired from his job as director of a youth project for a Denver poverty program, he immediately founded the Crusade for Justice. Its members were soon in the streets marching against discrimination, police brutality, and the Vietnam War.

Meanwhile, a four-year-old nonviolent Mexican-American struggle in New Mexico to obtain recognition of land titles guaranteed by the 1848 Treaty of Guadalupe Hidalgo was making national headlines. Reies López

Tijerina, an Assembly of God preacher, and 350 members of the Federal Alliance of Land Grants occupied ancestral lands inside the Kit Carson National Forest. Sentenced to two years in jail, Tijerina was placed on probation. The next year he led a sensational raid on the Tierra Amarilla courthouse. A jury cleared Tijerina of charges stemming from the raid, but Tijerina's renewed attempts to occupy the National Forest earned him a three-year jail sentence, and status as one of the nation's leading political prisoners.

Inspired by these rural struggles for justice, younger Mexican Americans in urban communities began calling themselves Chicanos to express the new militancy and to distinguish themselves from the go-slow, assimilationist hyphenated "Mexican-Americans."[7] They launched a Chicano political party, La Raza Unida ("United Race"). Assisted by the more moderate two-year-old Mexican American Legal Defense and Education Fund (MALDEF), La Raza Unida elected Chicano majorities to city councils and school boards in Crystal City and nearby towns in south Texas in 1970. Party members conducted classes to teach themselves and their children about their roots in *la raza*—the race of Mexicans and Native Americans who had resisted subjugation since the Spanish and U.S. conquests.[8]

Chicanos also organized a 5,000-strong self-defense militia of young women and men called the Brown Berets. One of their manifestos proclaimed: "We are against violence. . . . We have gone to the courts. . . . We have demonstrated peacefully . . . only to be met with more violence. . . . We have to arm ourselves now to protect ourselves."[9]

Inspired by the concept of *la raza*, some 10,000 Chicano high school students in East Los Angeles in early 1968 stunned the nation by walking out of their classrooms to protest run-down schools and racist teaching.

They demanded more Chicano staff. Lawmen rushed to their schools, beat them, and arrested those not fast enough to escape. Scapegoated for what came to be called the "high school blowouts" were the Brown Berets, who had little to do with the spontaneous protests. After court cases against blowout leaders dragged on for years at great expense, the charges against them were found to be unconstitutional. They had been exercising their First Amendment rights of free speech. During the next two years, similar "blowouts" occurred in almost every major Mexican-American barrio of the nation.

In 1969 the First National Chicano Youth Liberation Conference convened in Denver. Thousands attended and drafted El Plan Espiritual de Aztlán ("Spiritual Plan of Aztlán"—presumed name of the pre-Mexico, pre-U.S. lands). The plan called for community self-determination and celebration of Mexican Americans' roots. In Santa Barbara, California, college students merged their organizations into El Movimiento Estudiantil Chicano de Aztlán (MECHA—"The Chicano Student Movement of Aztlán").

This cultural nationalism, known as *Chicanismo,* flourished. Chicano publications, theater, dance, and art were born. Talented untrained teenage artists "muralized"—painted murals on—freeway pilings and barrio or college walls. Dozens of "underground" newspapers like Milwaukee's *La Guardia* appeared on the streets.[10]

Puerto Ricans were moving in a similar direction. Puerto Rican young men and women belonging to gangs in Chicago founded the Young Lords. Young Lords Field Marshal "Cosmo" told a magazine reporter: "What we had to realize was that it wasn't no good fightin' each other, but that what we were doing as a gang had to be against the capitalist institutions that are oppressing us." Politicized Chicano gang members echoed the sentiment. A bright-colored barrio wall mural by Los Angeles youngsters portrayed two members of rival gangs shaking hands before a backdrop of a clenched fist, the UFW's flag, and the words *Viva Mi Tierra* ("Long Live My Land").[11]

Young Lords chapters rapidly spread from Chicago. In Milwaukee the first Young Lords leaders came from boxing gymnasiums and street-corner hangouts.[12] In New York City the Young Lords Party (YLP) grew out of the Sociedad Albizu Campos, a group of students and college dropouts. The YLP's program called for Puerto Rican independence, equality for women, "a true education of our Afro-Indio culture and Spanish language," immediate withdrawal from Vietnam, armed self-defense, and "a socialist society."[13]

The Young Lords set up "people's health clinics" and occupied neighborhood churches, converting their basements into day-care centers and using their kitchens for breakfast-for-children programs. In 1970 the YLP and a coalition of patients and health workers took over South Bronx's run-down Lincoln Hospital to provide better health care.[14]

Many Latino gangs were influenced by the Black Panthers, founded in Oakland, California, as an African-American self-defense group in 1967. Some Young Lords were originally Panthers or later joined the Panthers. Chicago's Young Lords formed a coalition with the Black Panthers and the Young Patriots. The Patriots were a politicized group of white young men and women who had moved to Chicago from the South's poverty-stricken Appalachian Mountains. They had been raised in a culture that honored the Confederate flag and looked down upon blacks. They had often been called "white trash" by other whites. The movements of the 1960s had changed their way of thinking.

Unfortunately, death stalked every effort toward interracial unity of the oppressed. Malcolm X was gunned down shortly after he formed an African-American political party and announced that he was willing to work with

92

antiracist white groups. Martin Luther King was assassinated after he linked the Civil Rights Movement with the Anti-War Movement and at the very moment he was in Memphis to support a garbage workers' strike. An assassin's bullets felled Senator Robert Kennedy *after* he stopped condoning FBI wiretaps on civil rights activists like King and gained overwhelming support among Latino and African-American voters in Democratic presidential primary elections.

In urban barrios, younger and older Latinos often worked together within movements for better schools. In 1967–69, New York's Puerto Ricans and African Americans, parents and children alike, sparked a citywide struggle against inequality in education that soon incorporated Asians and other nonwhites. Highly competitive, allegedly culturally biased examinations for admission to the tuition-free city university system had kept enrollments nearly all white. With grassroots community support, the students seized the City College of New York to demand and win an historic "open admissions" policy that provided a fairer chance for Latinos to attend college. This victory spread to other states as well. New York's Puerto Ricans also won a struggle to establish the nation's only bilingual college, Eugenio María de Hostos Community College, in the South Bronx.

Latinos won bilingual education and the bilingual ballot in 1974. The Supreme Court ruled that placing non-English-speaking students in the same curriculum as English-speaking ones was a denial of the basic right to equal education. It was an important legal victory, but little had changed in the daily lives of the vast majority of Latinos.[15]

The crisis in the cities had worsened. The children of millions of African Americans and Hispanics who had found employment during World War II and the Korean War searched for decent jobs and found none. The victories of the Civil Rights Movement made it possible for a significant minority to move into the middle class, but the vast majority were left behind in deteriorating slum neighborhoods. Inferior education in their underfunded, understaffed schools left them unprepared to compete for better jobs. With some industries automating and others moving overseas where unskilled labor was even cheaper, many Latinos and African Americans either tried to get along on the low wages paid in manual-labor services or became part of an army of permanently unemployed.

Often the only way to survive was to apply for welfare. But to qualify, a person had to prove there was no breadwinner living at home. This no-win situation caused many irregularly employed husbands to drift away, their pride already bruised by job discrimination. The rates of broken marriages escalated, a severe blow to Latino traditions of close-knit families. As low-rent apartments were replaced with high-rise, high-rent luxury buildings, homelessness among Latinos also worsened.

For Puerto Ricans, the effect was especially devastating. Census data revealed that ever since the late 1960s they were poorer and had more "female-headed households" than any other group. Puerto Rican and other Latina women joined African Americans and whites in organizing the National Welfare Rights Organization (NWRO). NWRO won a number of rules changes that improved the lives of welfare recipients. No longer could social workers come unannounced into the homes of their "clients," searching the premises to see if they had bought anything new. NWRO also helped win a federal legal-aid program that still exists.[16]

In the midst of so much misery the potential for explosion always lurked, as the nation learned during the urban riots or uprisings of the mid-1960s. Riots were sometimes triggered by a political event, like the assassination of Martin Luther King in 1968. More often, problems with the police started the trouble.

Many people complained that some of the police who

patrolled their neighborhoods were racists. They filed complaints of police brutality and called the uprisings a response to "police riots." Perhaps the most famous "police riot," officially recognized as such, was the brutal 1968 police attack on antiwar protestors outside the Democratic Party national convention in Chicago, witnessed by millions of TV viewers.

The first Latino urban uprising was the June 1966 Division Street Riot in Chicago in response to a policeman's shooting of a twenty-year-old Puerto Rican man. More Latino rioting followed, particularly in New Jersey cities, right into the 1970s. One Puerto Rican bystander expressed a widespread Latino feeling when he told a reporter covering the 1966 Division Street troubles: "Tell the police we are not supposed to be beaten up like animals. Till you show us you are going to do something to stop this, this thing can't stop because we are human beings."[17]

In early 1968 a National Advisory Commission on Civil Disorders issued a widely publicized report that found white racism "essentially responsible" for urban riots. The nation was "moving toward two societies, one black, one white—separate and unequal." The report concluded that riots would always occur so long as the underlying economic causes of poverty were not corrected.

In an effort to stem the uprisings, federally funded antipoverty programs provided some job training and jobs for African Americans, Latinos, and Asian Americans. Title II of the 1964 Economic Opportunity Act developed "CAPs"—Community Action Programs—intended to assist local antipoverty efforts. With the U.S. government pouring millions of dollars into financing the Vietnam War, the programs were never sufficiently funded to make a major dent in poverty. In 1968 a Poor People's Encampment in Washington, D.C., planned by King shortly before his murder, drew 50,000 people. They protested the nation's failure to eradicate slums and demanded either jobs or a guaranteed annual income for every American. Tijerina led a Chicano contingent.

But neither adequate permanent funding to combat poverty nor sufficient new jobs were ever forthcoming. As King often repeated in the last years of his life, civil rights legislation did not cost a penny. It would take billions of dollars to eradicate poverty.

The situation worsened in the 1970s as what came to be called the "deindustrialization of America" went into high gear.[18] Automobile plants in Detroit, steel mills in Pittsburgh, and manufacturing plants from coast to coast shut down or moved away to areas of even cheaper labor. Parents no longer could tell a son or daughter hanging around street corners with their gang to "go down to the plant and get a job." White workers found themselves applying for welfare when their unemployment insurance ran out. For the first time, some of them started to sympathize with the Latinos and African Americans they met on unemployment lines.

The average age of a gang member crept upwards, until by the 1980s there were even father-son (mother-daugher) gang networks. For unemployed and school dropout youth from broken families, the gangs became their families. A gang member sent off to jail could count on his "family" on the outside. From 1970 to 1985, Hispanic prisoners were the fastest-growing group in the prison system, accounting for 27 percent of New York State's inmates and even more in California and Texas. Usually, they were tried by all-white juries, despite the earlier court victories of civil rights groups. One Anglo lawyer in Dallas noted in the mid-1970s that in a dozen years of practice he had never seen one Hispanic on a jury.[19]

Most Latino prisoners were accused of selling drugs. It was an irresistable temptation for some. A couple of drug sales to usually middle-class customers could bring far more than the income from a welfare check or a scarce low-paying job. The situation has worsened over time.

In 1971 politicized prisoners of all races and nationalities took control of one of four yards at Attica prison in upstate New York. To protect themselves until their modest demands for improved prison conditions were met, they held some guards hostage and invited in news reporters. A Southern white reporter, Tom Wicker of *The New York Times,* wrote: "The racial harmony that prevailed among the prisoners—it was absolutely astonishing. . . . That prison yard was the first place I have ever seen where there was no racism."[20] After five days of forward-moving negotiations, Governor Nelson Rockefeller ordered a surprise military assault on the Attica yard's prisoners. A hail of bullets killed forty, including nine guards.

By the early 1970s, several activists, realizing that unity among the poorest groups would strengthen their stuggles, were using the term *Latino* to identify their common struggle. Contacts were made between different groups at the huge demonstrations against the Vietnam War. College students, most of them white, were given exemptions from the draft while they were studying. Most Latinos were not so lucky. Some of them, jobless and hopeless, volunteered to join the military in order to get three meals a day. Latinos suffered 19 percent of the war's U.S. casualties, four times their percentage in the general population.[21]

Even the shooting of demonstrators—in which several white students at Kent State University, in Ohio, and black students at Jackson State University, in Mississippi, were killed in May 1970—did not deter the rising tide of opposition to the war. The following August, tens of thousands gathered for the "Chicano Moratorium" against the war, in Los Angeles. Police assaulted families picnicking at the rally. The "police riot" bloodied hundreds and left three dead. At a nearby bar, a police tear-gas canister killed television news reporter Rubén Salazar. Salazar had been running a series of shows exposing police brutality. No officer was punished.[22]

In order to concentrate on the economic problems, Chicanos and Puerto Ricans united in 1971 to launch Chicago's Spanish Coalition for Jobs and the Latino Institute. The Coalition won some jobs for Latinos under federal affirmative action programs based on the 1964 Civil Rights Act. The law made it mandatory for any business receiving government funding to hire some minority workers. Once again, some Latinos with high school or college degrees were able to find career jobs not open to them before.

But for poorer nonwhites to benefit from affirmative action proved almost as difficult as it was for them to obtain "fair and open housing" under the Fair Housing Act. Often a company would hire only one or two nonwhites "for show." It was even not unusual for one and the same person to be hired to meet two and sometimes even three categories of affirmative action. Hiring a dark-skinned Latina woman could, after all, fill the company's requirements for women, Hispanics, *and* blacks. Affirmative action was rarely enforced after 1980. For example, the percentage of nonwhites in New York's construction industry actually declined. Even those lucky few Latinos, African Americans, and women who found better jobs were paid less than whites and males doing the same work.[23]

With the winding down of the Vietnam War and most people scrambling to survive during the severe economic recessions that followed, the movements for social justice dwindled and came under increasing government attack. At least one police agent confirmed there were plots to assassinate Cesar Chavez. The government's COINTELPRO, short for Counter Intelligence Program, had a 1966 Puerto Rican component whose name reflected its aim: "Operation Chaos." YLP Minister of Information Pablo "Yoruba" Guzmán later summed up the consequences: "Many left the ranks; leaders were jailed; cynicism and mistrust set in."[24] Brown Beret founder David Sanchez, a former chairman of the Los Angeles Mayor's Youth Council, announced the disbanding of the

Brown Berets in late 1972 because of the large number of police informants inside the organization.[25]

Phones were tapped and homes were bugged in order to listen in on activists' planning sessions or to gather information on leaders for FBI "dirty tricks operations." Federal agents joined Latino and African-American groups as double agents and planted drugs in activists' cars or homes, wrote false, incriminating letters, and encouraged internal fights. Sometimes lawmen resorted to outright murder, as in the case of the police killings of Chicago's Fred Hampton and other Black Panthers. Grand juries indicted scores of leaders, often on unconstitutional grounds. Most urban police forces had a "Red Squad" dedicated to hounding protesters. There were dozens of beatings, shootings, and murders of Latinos, which were later documented by the U.S. Commission on Civil Rights. More than one historian compared the political repression with the persecution of immigrants and union members after 1917 and during the post-World War II Cold War era.[26]

Once again it was "blame the victim" time, as white racists pointed their fingers at the programs for minorities as the cause of increased white unemployment. The emerging sentiment helped elect the ultraconservative Ronald Reagan to the presidency. During the Reagan and Bush years (1981–93) most of the programs created earlier in favor of civil rights and economic opportunity were emasculated.

But something important had happened. It was more difficult after the sixties for racists and sexists to openly act on their beliefs. The Anti-War Movement had won over a majority of the voters, helping to bring about withdrawal from Vietnam. It would make it more difficult in the future to send young men and women off to die in questionable foreign wars. The sixties had taught thousands of people how to use their right to free speech to organize. They would use that new knowledge in the days ahead.

7
siete

YEARNING TO BREATHE FREE: REFUGEES AND IMMIGRANTS

Here life is not worth
a rotten guava.
If a hoodlum doesn't kill you
the factory will.
> — Verse from a merengue
>   (popular Dominican music)[1]

When you said that you were
a Cuban, it sounded like a magic
word that opened every door.
> — Cuban refugee, 1966[2]

On July 1, 1986, the day of sentencing, the eight convicted felons walked up the steps of the courthouse building in Tucson, Arizona. They were ministers, priests, nuns, and lay workers in churches along the U.S.-Mexico border.

They noticed that someone had draped on the building's wall a banner with the Statue of Liberty verse "Give me your tired, your poor, your huddled masses yearning to breathe free." In their eyes, they had been branded criminals because they had acted according to the Statue's credo. They had opened the doors of their churches and homes to Central-American refugees fleeing military repression. The army had destroyed some 500 Indian villages in Guatemala and killed nearly 100,000 people. In El Salvador the story was similar. Millions were still trying to escape, becoming part of the hemisphere's largest flight from horror in history. But the Immigration and Naturalization Service (INS) claimed the refugees were economic, not political, and loaded them on airplanes that returned them to the terror and warfare at home.

"Death flights" were what the eight called them. And they were not alone in this opinion. Supporting them were 100,000 activists in their Sanctuary Movement. It was America's newest underground railroad, larger even than the one conducted a century and a half earlier by the Abolitionists to protect runaway slaves. It spirited Central American refugees into safe houses away from the vans and helicopters of *la migra* (the INS). In a letter to the trial judge, Earl H. Carroll, forty-seven members of the U.S. Congress commended the eight's humanitarian service.

After eighteen weeks the eight were convicted of "conspiracy" to "smuggle, protect, or harbor aliens" and "illegals."[3] It was hard for supporters of the Sanctuary Movement to accept these bizarre labels for the Central-American refugees. They were human beings, not aliens from another planet. Furthermore, a person can commit an illegal act, but can a person be "an illegal"?

Now, taking their seats in the courtroom for their sentencing, the defendants at last had their chance to speak. Margaret "Peggy" J. Hutchison, a slim intense twenty-seven-year-old social service worker for the United Methodist Church, rose and adjusted her round granny glasses over her intense brown eyes. "I stand before this court to proclaim 'never again,'" she declared.[4] Her use of the famous Jewish vow was common among defenders of Latin-American political refugees. The people they were protecting were being denied asylum just as Jews had been turned away during the Holocaust, told that the "quotas" were filled.

Reverend John Fife, a tall, lanky forty-year-old pastor of the Presbyterian Church in Tucson's southside barrio, informed the judge about the fifteen-year-old boy he had helped. The boy's family had been butchered in El Salvador, where the U.S.-aided army's motto was "Be a patriot, kill a priest." Said Reverend Fife: "If this was one of my boys, what would I want the church to do? I had no choice. None of us had any choice."[5]

Next, Sister Darlene Nicgorski told the judge that she had served in a Guatemalan town where a death squad had shot and killed the local priest and his driver after an evening mass. Death squads were "unofficial" bands of military officers and right-wing goons who terrorized human rights workers and unarmed civilians, calling them all communists. Sister Nicgorski told one reporter: "I kept thinking about the people I knew who had never even heard of a Communist. They just wanted teachers, health care, some land to grow crops."[6]

Judge Carroll sentenced the eight to three- to five-years' probation, a far lighter punishment than other Sanctuary participants had received.

From the point of view of all who supported the eight defendants, there were several glaring contradictions between law and reality. At the height of the Civil Rights Movement in 1964–65, when Congress revised immigration laws to modify the racially biased national-origins quota system, it emphasized political refuge as one of three immigration criteria.[7]

Yet as thousands of Salvadoran, Guatemalan, Honduran, and Nicaraguan men, women, and children fled north to escape the warfare engulfing Central America, INS authorities rounded them up and placed them in barbed-wire-enclosed detention camps. The camps sprang up in Arizona, Texas, California, Colorado, Florida, Louisiana, even New York. Sometimes Mexican "undocumented" migrant workers were thrown in with the Central Americans. Hundreds of children were also placed behind barbed wire. Latinos, concerned clergy, and human rights groups like Americas Watch and Amnesty International decried the camps.[8]

During the so-called contra war in Nicaragua, it became apparent that a political double standard was being used by the U.S. government to interpret political refuge provisions of the immigration laws. The contras were U.S.-commanded supporters of Nicaraguan dictator Anastasio Somoza, Jr., who had been overthrown by the Sandinista revolution of 1979. They were invading Nicaragua from U.S.-built bases in neighboring Central-American countries. They were cheered on by the majority of the new Nicaraguan residents in the United States, people of wealth recognized as political refugees fleeing the revolution.

Most settled in Miami's Sweetwater district, rebaptized "Little Managua." Then, as the contras' warfare ravaged Nicaragua, taking some 50,000 lives, poorer darker-skinned Nicaraguans began showing up. They were fleeing the violence. Many of them had seen their unarmed families or friends murdered by contra land mines, poisoned wells, or outright massacres. Only 14 percent of the new Nicaraguans filing for political asylum received it. The rest couldn't convince authorities that they supported the contras.[9]

A televised event centering on the contra issue struck many as evidence of even more hypocrisy in high places. Just months after the Tucson sentencing, the televised "Iran-contragate" hearings in Congress clearly exposed the illegal U.S. government actions in Central America. Evidence had come to light that the Reagan administration had been selling missiles to Iran and then using the proceeds to fund shipments of weapons to the Nicaraguan contras, in direct violation of 1982 legislation prohibiting the continued arming of the contras. Journalists further discovered that some of the arms-delivering planes had returned from Central America loaded with cocaine. Its sale provided another source of illicit contra funding. Meanwhile the administration was conducting a massive "Just say no" campaign against drugs!

Congress's hearings revealed that the administration had drawn up plans to suspend the Constitution and use already constructed "detention centers" as holding pens for up to 400,000 expected protesters in the event of a direct U.S. invasion of Nicaragua. President Reagan had no intention of allowing the kind of demonstrations that had forced his friend Richard Nixon to pull out of Vietnam in 1975. The demonstrators' rallies, including a 1981 march on Washington against a short-lived proposal to reinstate the military draft, had pressured Congress to ban military support for the contras in the first place.

Despite government threats and harassment, the anti-interventionist movement kept growing. More than 1,000 "solidarity" organizations blossomed to defend human rights. Some towns proclaimed themselves sister cities with Nicaraguan towns, collecting money and supplies for the Sandinistas and war refugees. In 1984 Latinos in Los Angeles marched outside the site of the summer Olympics shouting "Hands Off Nicaragua!" and "Hell

No, We Won't Go!" They were announcing their refusal to go to Central America to join U.S. soldiers working with death-squad militaries and the contras.

With many nations opposing U.S. intervention in Nicaragua, the World Court in 1986 censured the United States for mining Nicaragua's harbors and instructing the contras in "acts contrary to general principles of humanitarian law." A CIA pamphlet taught the contras that killing teachers and farmers would demoralize the pro-Sandinista Nicaraguans and weaken their revolution. Echoing the Court, former CIA director Stansfield Turner called U.S. policy "state-sponsored terrorism."

Over the next few years, huge marches in Washington, D.C., and San Francisco protested U.S. policies in Central America and South Africa. In 1988 Latino veterans joined a "Vietnam Veterans' Convoy" of thirty-seven trucks that overcame U.S. government harassment to deliver food, medicine, and clothing to the Nicaraguan people. That same year, an INS investigation of the shooting of a Mexican national inside Mexican territory by a U.S. Border Patrol officer concluded that agents had every right to shoot into Mexico against such provocations as rock throwing. A newly created Alien Border Control Commission brought together agents of the INS, FBI, CIA, and Justice Department to coordinate mass internments.[10]

Pressured by the independent protest movement at home and diplomatic censure abroad, the U.S. government finally agreed to peace negotiations in Central America. The United Nations sent a military peacekeeping mission to the region in 1989. But the slaughter in El Salvador and Guatemala continued. After the Sanctuary Movement won a court case against the INS, the government introduced a temporary sanctuary program in 1991 for Salvadorans—another major victory for the anti-interventionist movement.[11]

The grave troubles in Central America had begun shortly after the Cuban Revolution of 1959. Fearful of losing power in their own countries as the dictator Batista and his army had in Cuba, U.S.-backed armies in Latin America ushered in a "long dark night of state-sponsored terror."[12] Democratic institutions were eliminated, millions of people were jailed, and U.S. corporations were assured plenty of nonunion workers and favorable terms of investment in Latin America. Runaway shops became an everyday expression used to describe factories that closed down in the United States and reopened south of the border.

Starting in the early 1960s in the Dominican Republic and spreading from there, death squads and military personnel systematically "disappeared" (kidnapped) and killed more than 200,000 prodemocracy civilians in Latin America. Little wonder many, including nearly half of Uruguay's population, fled!

The 1990 U.S. Census reported nearly twenty million foreign-born residents, most of them from Latin America and Asia. Millions of "undocumented workers"—immigrants without legal papers—went uncounted. The Census Bureau estimates their number to be four to five million. Yet compared with other industrialized countries, the United States still has a low percentage of foreign-born.

Taking into account those persons missed by census takers, there were probably more than a million Dominicans, a million Salvadorans, and close to half a million Guatemalans living in the United States by 1990. Their newly settled barrios crisscrossed the nation—New York, greater Washington, D.C., Chicago, Miami, Houston, San Francisco–Oakland. Los Angeles was said to be the site of the world's second largest Salvadoran population, estimated at half a million. Political turmoil in their home countries as well as starvation had forced them to leave their homes. Many of them believed that the problems in their countries had been caused in large part by U.S. policies favoring dictatorial governments, as we saw in the 1954 Guatemala–United Fruit story in Chapter 4.

Some immigrants from the Dominican Republic, who now outnumbered Cuban Americans, considered themselves political refugees, although denied that status by the U.S. government. They arrived after the 1963 military coup against President Juan Bosch and the Marine invasion that prevented Bosch's return to power in 1965. They were joined by others after disputed elections in the Dominican Republic in the 1970s.

Nearly half of the Dominicans settled in New York City. The largest Dominican barrio is in Washington Heights, a fifty-block zone of upper Manhattan, "one of [the nation's] most depressed areas."[13] The majority are here legally, obtaining temporary student visas or entering under the family reunification or skilled worker provisions of the immigration laws. Because it became widely known that immigration authorities rarely accept political refugees from tyrannical governments the U.S supports, few Dominicans applied under the political refugee statutes. As U.S. authorities began rejecting more applicants for regular visas (80 percent in 1990), the number of "illegal" Dominican immigrants notably increased.

Unscrupulous U.S. employers quickly harnessed their nonunionized labor under slavelike conditions in aging factories, apparel sweatshops, or restaurants and hotels. The merengue verse at the opening of this chapter expresses their despair.

Growing numbers of Dominicans are "boat people" —desperate economic refugees braving the shark-ridden waters of the Mona Passage to Puerto Rico in flimsy vessels. Ten percent of them drown or die of exposure during the crossing, and another 60 percent are deported from Puerto Rico. Some manage to remain in Puerto Rico, while others fly into the United States posing as Puerto Ricans.

Dominicans, like Colombians, have been scapegoated for drug trafficking. The few Dominicans who are involved are usually at the bottom of the drug pyramid, dealing crack cocaine on the street. In 1992 a policeman's fatal shooting of a suspected Dominican drug runner in New York City's Washington Heights led to explosive rioting. Several Dominican civic organizations helped calm the situation. Dominican social justice advocates like the decade-old Alianza de Dominicanos Progresistas ("Alliance of Progressive Dominicans") won recognition of the need for better police and other public services in the barrio. But a police killing of a Dominican bicyclist in the summer of 1993 increased the tension. Dominican city councilman Guillermo Linares was the neighborhood's elected voice at City Hall.

Chilean refugees in the United States also left home after a U.S.-encouraged military takeover. After Chile's people in 1970 elected Salvador Allende as their president, he nationalized (with compensation) U.S. copper holdings, just as Arbenz had tried to nationalize United Fruit's unused land in 1954. Secretary of State Henry Kissinger said: "I don't see why we need to stand by and watch [Chile] go Communist due to the irresponsibility of its own people."[14] Allende was a parliamentary socialist like those who have governed such countries as England, France, and Holland.

The U.S.-backed coup in 1973 toppled Allende and arrested, tortured, or slaughtered thousands. Women were even arrested for wearing slacks or blue jeans, for in the eyes of the new dictator, General Augusto Pinochet, such clothing was a sure sign of communist affiliation!

Those who lived through Pinochet's purge fled for their lives. Knowing that they would not be granted status as political refugees in the United States, some Chileans obtained student and professional visas with the help of American friends.

Immigrants from other South American countries were also frequently fleeing violence in their homelands. According to the 1990 Census, Colombians composed about 40 percent of South America's one million immigrants, followed by Peruvians, Ecuadorans, and Argentines. Many Colombians settled in the borough of Queens in New York City. There were more middle-class people among South America's immigrants than among those from Central America or the Dominican Republic. Except for some who participated in the anti-interventionist movement, most South Americans did not become deeply involved in social justice causes here.

Panamanians experienced a direct U.S. invasion of their country in 1989. The stated purpose was to capture dictator Manuel Noriega and try him for narcotics trafficking. Yet many people knew that earlier, when Noriega had worked for the CIA, the Drug Enforcement Administration (DEA) had praised his work in combatting drug smuggling.

Some Panamanians spoke at anti-interventionist rallies like the overflow meeting at New York City's Town Hall, where they described U.S. bombings of Panama City's working-class neighborhoods. They helped independent investigators like former U.S. attorney general Ramsey Clark and concerned Hollywood filmmakers document the truth.

One result was *The Panama Deception,* winner of the 1992 Academy Award for the Best Documentary. According to the film (and most experts on Panama), the actual mission of the invasion was to reassert U.S. control over Central America and restore to power the traditional "twenty families" that had ruled Panama prior to 1968. This would assure Washington that in the year 2000, when the 1977–78 Canal Treaties would give Panama sovereignty over the Panama Canal, the "right" people, friendly to U.S. business, would be in charge. Many opponents of the "twenty families" had resided in the bombed-out neighborhoods. No Panamanian with any sense at all attempted to enter the United States as a political refugee from U.S. aggression![15]

The Cuban refugee story is a study in contrasts. In

1959 most of the 70,000 middle-class and working-class Cubans already living here welcomed the reforms introduced by the man whose speeches they adored, "El Caballo"—Fidel Castro (see Chapter 4). But they soon found themselves outnumbered by hundreds of thousands of more affluent, mostly white Cuban exiles, many of whom were followers of the deposed dictator Batista. The government's Cuban Refugee Program provided the new arrivals with over $1 billion in assistance. Cubans were offered relaxed citizenship requirements, small-business loans, help in job placement, relocation expenses to other cities, scholarships, health care, and, in Florida, bilingual education as early as 1960.

With all of this aid, the anti-Castro Cubans were able to create what they later called the "golden exile" enclave known as Little Miami. Years later, one of them recalled: "When you said that you were a Cuban, it sounded like a magic word that opened every door. Employers demonstrated their willingness towards Cubans. . . . Landlords gladly rented out their apartments. . . . Colleges and universities started to hire Cuban professors, and adolescents in the high schools were winners of outstanding awards."[16]

Naturally, Puerto Ricans, other Latinos, and African Americans resented losing out to the favored Cuban refugees in the competition for jobs. Riots fueled by unemployment and anti-Cuban backlash erupted in Miami's predominantly black Liberty City in the early 1980s.

By the mid-1990s Cubans numbered more than a million, or about 4 percent of the nation's Hispanics. A minority of the Cuban refugees' children, who were adults by the 1970s or 1980s, publicly complained about U.S. racism and the heartless U.S. economic blockade of Cuba. They launched a literary magazine called *Areito* and sought to end the blockade and reestablish U.S.-Cuban diplomatic relations. They even met with Cuban president Castro and persuaded him to ease travel restrictions for refugee families (without any corresponding change in the U.S. restrictions that had been imposed on travel to Cuba right after the revolution). Some of these peacemaking Cuban Americans were—and are—terrorized, even killed, by ultrarightist Cuban exile groups.[17]

The right-wing terrorists gradually lost support in the Cuban communities of Florida, New York, New Jersey, and Illinois. Their reputations suffered when people learned of their roles in the Watergate burglary of the Democratic Party's national headquarters that led to President Nixon's resignation; the 1975 blowing up of a Cuban civilian airliner in which all seventy-three aboard were killed; and the 1976 car-bombing murder on Embassy Row in Washington of Chile's ex-foreign minister Orlando Letelier and his American research assistant Ronnie Moffit.

As the years passed, growing numbers of Cuban Americans, critical of the blockade's hard-line approach to the Cuban people, began sending food and money to their relatives, especially after the cutoff in aid from the former communist nations of Europe. In 1992 the UN General Assembly called for an end to the thirty-two-year-old trade embargo against Cuba.

Cuban Americans are no longer—if they ever were —a united, conservative, pro-Republican Party bloc. Some are particularly proud of the revolution's reversal of racism. Few deny Cuba's world-renowned gains in education, health care, and housing (there are no homeless). More and more call for a negotiated end to the Cold War against Cuba.

In an effort to meet criticisms of its failures to admit *non-Cuban* Latin-American political *refugees*, Congress passed the Refugee Act of 1980 that redefined *refugee* to conform with the UN protocol providing refuge for *anyone* having a "well-founded fear of persecution." Right after the Act was passed, some 125,000 "boat people" from Cuba (affectionately called "the Marielitos") were given a rousing welcome. But thousands of black refugees fleeing Haiti's brutal dictatorship were still being detained on the high seas, deported, or thrown into "detention centers" described by the mass media as virtual concentration camps. President Reagan's 1981 Task Force on Immigration and Refugee Policy warned that "detention could create an appearance of 'concentration camps' filled largely by blacks." Yet the 1980 Refugee Act was soon modified to provide loopholes for continued discrimination.

Central Americans hoped for fair treatment in the United States. Up to 300,000 resided in the Maryland-Virginia-Washington, D.C., area, site of the nation's oldest Salvadoran community. Many of them were women who worked as maids and babysitters for government bureaucrats and foreign embassy personnel. They had seen brutality at home and were unlikely to put up with it in "the land of the free." When in 1991 a thirty-year-old Salvadoran immigrant was critically wounded in the latest of a series of police shootings, the community's Latinos and African Americans rioted for three nights. Two years later, a report by the U.S. Commission on Civil Rights confirmed that the Washington area's Latinos were the victims of police "abuse, harassment, and misconduct."[18]

During the disturbances a number of respected community leaders emerged. One of them, a Salvadoran, became director of the Central American Refugee Center (CARECEN) and then founded a minority-rights empowerment organization to fight for respect and improved housing and health services. One of its initial victories occurred in Arlington, Virginia.

Every morning Salvadorans in Arlington were harassed by the city police as they gathered at a designated street corner to wait for employers to drive up and collect them for work on construction jobs or as gardeners and maids. A half block away was a public park, which had its own police force and therefore was off limits for the city cops. The new empowerment organization won the right to set up a trailer in the park providing informational services. Peace returned, and unemployment and other problems were handled smoothly at the trailer. Similar struggles emerged in the newest Salvadoran communities created in Seattle, Boston, and several smaller cities. The participants were mostly youth fleeing military conscription and El Salvador's escalated warfare of the late 1980s.[19]

In California, Mexicans remained the largest group of immigrants. Congress's decision to end the Bracero Program in 1965 did not deter the flow of Mexican workers northward. Counting "illegals," some four million Mexicans came to the United States in the 1980s.[20] Until passage of the 1986 Immigration Reform and Control Act (IRCA), Congress had honored employers' needs to keep the border doors revolving by refusing to pass bills "sanctioning" (fining) employers who hired "undocumented" workers. IRCA's provisions for employers' sanctions were difficult to enforce. With recession cutbacks everywhere, it was impossible to beef up the INS staff needed for such a large operation. Most employers continued to hire Latinos, but some, wanting to avoid unexpected raids by the INS and IRCA's paperwork hassle, turned away even Latinos who were citizens. Hispanic unemployment rates climbed faster than African-American ones the year after IRCA's passage.[21]

Strangely, it was actually employers' needs for more cheap immigrant labor that helped IRCA become law. Projected labor shortfalls of seven million fewer young workers entering the labor force each decade led *Business Week* to conclude in its June 23, 1980, issue: "The U.S. will need immigrants to buttress the labor supply if the economy is to grow." In IRCA's fine print was a contract labor provision permitting the importation of up to a third of a million or more foreign (Mexican) workers a year, mainly in agriculture but also in other areas as needed.

Contract labor, outlawed a century earlier, was back. Young people of Mexican descent were projected as second only to young whites as the largest source of new entrants into the labor force by the year 2000.[22]

The economic downturns of the 1970s and early 1980s and early 1990s led to fresh nativist outbursts scapegoating Mexicans and other Latinos for "taking American jobs."[23] Actually, except for some African Americans, who are always "the last hired and first fired," very few Americans wanted the jobs that Latinos accepted. The INS raided workplaces during the 1982 recession, searching for and detaining thousands of "illegals," in an action called "Operation Jobs". There were, however, few job applicants for the positions newly vacated by the arrested Latinos.[24] According to surveys of the INS itself, most immigrants held unskilled, low-wage jobs unacceptable to most Americans. Immigrants averaged ten- to fourteen-hour workdays. Latina women were even more exploited.

Most economists believe that the new immigrants, like earlier ones, are *helping* the economy. As the business newspaper *The Wall Street Journal* reported on June 18, 1976, "Legal or not, the present wave of [illegal] Western Hemisphere immigrants may well be providing the margin of survival for entire sectors of the economy." The *Journal*'s May 7, 1985, headline added: "Illegal Immigrants Are Backbone of Economy in States of Southwest—They Make Computer Parts, Package Arthritis Pills, Cook, Clean and Baby-Sit—Prisoners in the Bunkhouse."

For one thing, immigrants contribute much more money to the economy than they take out. A 1979 Labor Department study revealed that over 75 percent of "undocumented workers" pay Social Security and income taxes, but only 0.5 percent ever receive welfare benefits, and only 1 percent use food stamps. The same workers' contributions account for a significant chunk of the hard-pressed Social Security trust fund—up to $80 billion a year. A 1984 Ford Foundation report confirms that "As more whites reach Social Security age, their support will depend on Social Security taxes paid by an increasingly Hispanic and black workforce."[25]

Most Americans never hear about the *Wall Street Journal* or Labor Department findings. As in the past, the latest anti-immigrant hysteria has been fueled by the mass media.[26] A "brown scare" in the late 1970s was stimulated considerably by former CIA director William Colby's widely quoted statement in interviews for *Playboy* magazine and the *Los Angeles Times* in June 1978. Colby claimed that Mexican immigration represented a greater long-term threat to the United States than the Soviet Union. Ronald Reagan was elected to the presidency in 1980 on a platform of promising "to regain control of our borders"—an obvious impossibility unless he ordered the building of a 2,000-mile-long "Berlin Wall" topped by electric fencing!

Some Hispanics fought back against the frightening nativist offensive. In 1980, community and labor organizers on both sides of the border circulated a thirteen-article Bill of Rights for the Undocumented Worker, emphasizing international human rights and fair treatment of labor. A National Chicano Immigration Conference followed, bringing together hundreds of Mexican and Latino organizations in a joint effort to abolish all forms of contract labor and the Border Patrol.[27]

Most of the participants in the conference knew that they were up against a tidal wave of racism, especially in areas with large populations of Latinos. California was one such place. Home to half the nation's immigrants, California in the 1980s and 1990s resembled not so much a melting pot as a boiling cauldron. Long before flames consumed large sections of Los Angeles in 1992 (after an all-white Simi Valley, California, jury acquitted four policemen on trial for the brutal clubbing of African-

American motorist Rodney King), racism against Mexican Americans had escalated. Year after year, police sweeps, carried out in the name of conducting a "war on drugs" and "controlling the gangs," terrified impoverished urban neighborhoods. Workplace roundups of so-called illegal aliens by INS agents intimidated all Latinos. The annual number of deportees zipped past one million. According to an attorney for the Los Angeles-based National Center for Immigrants' Rights, up to a third of the deportees were not even legally deportable in the first place.[28]

The U.S.-Mexico border became a veritable war zone, pitting unarmed migrant workers against the Border Patrol as well as roaming bands of Ku Klux Klansmen. Reports of shootings increased. On April 18, 1985, INS border patrolmen gunned down and critically wounded a twelve-year-old Mexican boy near San Ysidro, California. Local television stations in San Diego County reported that white suburban teenagers were following their example by shooting at Mexicans "for sport."

In the years leading up to the Simi Valley verdict, police shootings and beatings of nonwhites escalated. Several "blue ribbon" commission reports highlighted serious problems in police-community relations. The Christopher Commission Report on the Los Angeles Police Department reproduced hundreds of what it called "brazen and extensive [police] references to beatings and other excessive uses of force." It cited computer messages "sent to and from patrol cars throughout the city over the units' Mobile Digital Terminals (MDTs)." Typical were the following: "Sounds like monkey slapping time," "We're huntin' wabbits," "I almost got me a Mexican last nite," "Capture him, beat him and treat him like dirt," "A full moon and a full gun make for a night of fun." Commission chairman Warren M. Christopher, later appointed U.S. secretary of state, emphatically declared: "This is a national problem."[29]

A 1991 report by a seventeen-member New York State Judicial Commission on Minorities concurred. It found "two justice systems at work."[30] Long before an amateur operator of a camcorder gave the TV media a videotape of King's beating (the Los Angeles Police Department had refused to accept the videotape), concerned Chicanos had been videotaping similar abuses of Latinos and delivering them to police commanders.

The rage of Latinos was as fierce as African-American anger during the storm that followed the jury acquittal of King's tormenters. Half the residents in Los Angeles' most heavily damaged neighborhoods were Latino. Half of those arrested were Latino. A third of businesses destroyed were Latino-owned.

After the fires had been put out, Los Angeles immigrant-rights groups and Latino politicians protested that Border Patrol agents had arrested many "undocumented" immigrants while searching their homes for looted goods. They also denounced the fact that the police had turned over many arrested immigrants to the INS, even though the immigrants normally would have been released for lack of evidence.[31]

The events in Los Angeles sent a message to Latinos all over the country. Major battles for social justice were still to come.

La Lucha Continua! ("The Struggle Goes On!")

I was frequently called a "spik."
I am no longer called a "spik."
I am now referred to as being
culturally deprived, socially
disadvantaged, and a product
of the culture of poverty.
> —Joseph Monserrat,
> middle-class
> Puerto Rican[1]

On a sunny April day in 1988, students from different racial and ethnic backgrounds filled a San Diego college classroom to overflowing. Since an immigrant worker had been a guest speaker the previous week, in the spirit of fairness a prominent local Mexican-American police officer, who had patrolled the border areas for many years, had been invited to give a guest lecture.

A number of young men and women whom the students had never seen before filled the usually vacant chairs in the last row and sat on the floor along the back wall. They were speaking to one another in Spanish and were all Latinos, although a few were very light complexioned and one had red hair.

As he spoke about his exploits, the large, plump uniformed officer strutted back and forth, occasionally patting his sidearm for emphasis. He concluded by expressing his hope that "minority students" in the room would consider him a role model.

Then he sat down next to some people who had accompanied him, all wearing civilian clothes. They vigorously nodded their approval and whispered something in his ear. He snickered.

During the question-and-answer period, the first to speak was the redheaded stranger. He explained to the class that he and the others in the back of the room were members of a local barrio gang who followed the officer wherever he spoke "like a truth squad."

"We are not impressed with this man as a role model," he said. "My 'manos ["brothers and sisters"] will tell you why."

The officers in front shifted nervously in their chairs.

One by one, each of the gang members detailed an incident he or she had witnessed where the guest speaker, without provocation, had shot or beat up immigrant workers or gang members.

The officer denied each charge. His companions yelled out things like "He wasn't even there that night" or "Why didn't you report this to the precinct?"

Within a few minutes, both groups were shouting.

A deep voice bellowed from the back of the room: "Wait a minute!"

Students spun around in their chairs to look.

There stood the new "TA" (teaching assistant). The previous TA, a Mexican American from a farmworker family, had taken a leave of absence from school to help his family pick the crops. The new TA was also a Mexican American. Barrel-chested, he stood well over six feet tall and looked as menacing as the policeman.

"I'm a trucker," the TA said. "My route takes me to Tijuana. I have just one question. How come you and your buddies stopped me at the border last Friday night, slammed me up against the wall, and beat the living sh-- out of me?"

Again, denials. The guest speaker stood up to leave, motioning his group to come with him.

"And you ask us why we don't report your crimes to the precinct—you gotta be kidding!" the TA shouted.

The room exploded with "Yeahs" and Spanish curses as the policeman walked quickly out of the room, flanked by his friends. His hand was on his sidearm.[2]

As the classroom scene suggested, the tensions in border cities had not abated. It was the same all over the nation. America's economy seemed stuck in low gear. Hoping to rev up the economy, the government had escalated the armaments race against the outgunned, outspent Soviet Union. This had helped bring the communist superpower to its knees, but it also had ballooned the federal budget deficit. With less federal funds sent their way, many cities were close to bankruptcy.

Those most affected by the subsequent cutbacks were the poor. Whenever budgets were cut, social welfare programs were the first to go. By the end of the "Reagan free market revolution" of the 1980s, when defense spending went through the roof, day-care centers had been closed and only a handful of antipoverty programs remained.

When the Cold War ended, many people called for a "peace dividend." They wanted sharp reductions in defense spending and new programs to rebuild America and put people to work. It was time, they urged, to construct new bridges, lay new railroad tracks, erect much needed low-cost and middle-income housing.

Instead, defense workers were laid off in greater numbers and hardly any new jobs were created. The deficit had to be reduced, critics were told, and everyone would have to tighten their belts. The problem was that America's working people already had their belts secured at the last notch. As decent-paying jobs went down the drain, people made negative jokes about their chances being limited to dead-end "McJobs," named after the fast-food chain McDonald's.

Living conditions among Latinos worsened as even low-paying jobs disappeared. Puerto Rican poverty levels in the 1990s reached 40.6 percent, compared with 31.9 percent for African Americans, 28.1 percent for all Latinos, and 10.7 percent for whites.[3]

Ignoring the vast majority of Latinos living in misery, the mass media emphasized the advances of a minority of Hispanics who had become professionals, managers, and politicians. *Time* magazine called the 1980s "The Decade of the Hispanics." The article was referring to the election of several Latinos to political office. Many Latinos knew that the headline was a gross exaggeration. Despite electing one governor and a few mayors and state and federal legislators, Latinos continued to be grossly underrepresented in the political system. In 1993, they held less than 1 percent of the nation's half million elected positions![4]

Even that small number of Latinos in public office seemed doomed to shrink. Most of their seats had been won by court decisions that reversed the kind of "redistricting" that had defeated Vito Marcantonio during the Cold War (see Chapter 5). Using the 1965 Voting Rights Act, Latinos and their supporters had won court-ordered redistricting measures to create voting districts that gave segregated Latinos and African Americans a fairer shot at political representation.

But even the token number of electoral victories for Latinos brought opponents into court. In 1993 a five-four Supreme Court decision threatened to end redistricting as a violation of the constitutional rights of white voters![5]

This legal defeat went unnoticed by most Latinos. The economic problems and reversal of other gains in the 1980s seemed more important. Most Latinos in cities like Los Angeles were disenfranchised anyway, because of the harsh day-to-day struggle for survival, immigrant status, or the absence of bilingual ballots. In the early 1980s the federal government had reduced the number of counties requiring bilingual ballots. In Los Angeles County, whose population is 35 percent Latino, the ballot existed only in English.

For Latinos the health and education of their children took priority over all other issues. Environmental hazards and inferior medical care contributed to deteriorating health in urban slums. Because poorer neighborhoods are often located closer to polluting industries, heavy automobile traffic, and dump sites, slum dwellers breathe in dirtier air than the people living in suburbs or better-off urban neighborhoods. Many Latinos following events in their home countries knew that U.S. producers of pesticides and other chemicals banned in the United States sometimes sold their products to nations with lax environmental laws. Poultry producers in the United States, for example, would inject young chickens with female hormones to speed their growth. When new government regulations limited the amount of hormones they could inject, producers shipped their overdosed poultry to Puerto Rico. No one knew about it until young Puerto Rican children showed up in doctors' offices with premature sexual development—the girls menstruating and the boys with swollen breasts from eating estrogen-laden chicken dinners![6]

It is a little known fact that Latinos are pioneers of environmentalism. Latino farmworkers helped spark the antipesticide fight in the 1950s that led to the banning of DDT. For six years before his death in 1993, Cesar Chavez (head of the UFW) led a grape boycott to end the use of toxic pesticides sprayed on crops. The pesticides were causing birth defects and high cancer rates among UFW members and affecting consumers as well. As a result of the boycott, some of the pesticides were discontinued in the early 1990s.[7]

In New York City in 1993, environmental and educational issues were joined together when New York City's schools were discovered to have exposed millions of students to cancer-causing asbestos because of faulty building inspections. The schools were shut down for repairs, but when they reopened, some were still unsafe. Parents and children, many of them Latinos and African Americans, demanded that the schools be made safe before the children would return to them.

Almost every gain of the sixties and seventies came under attack in the eighties and nineties—even the right to speak in the Spanish language in certain settings! Many Latinos were proud of the fact that they spoke two languages while most native-born Americans spoke only English. A white backlash tried to diminish that pride with campaigns against bilingualism. A successful "English Only" movement made English the "official language" in several states and counties.

Latinos, again because of their dreams for their children, have struggled to preserve bilingual education. In 1991 even an outspoken opponent of multicultural education, Linda Chavez, former head of the U.S. Civil Rights Commission under President Reagan, didn't like the idea of returning to the old days when children were forced "to sink or swim in classes in which they don't understand the language of instruction."[8]

Latinos are united on this issue. In 1993 they

achieved a significant victory. A Dade County (Miami) commission repealed a 1980 ordinance barring the county from conducting its business in any language other than English. Across the waters, in Puerto Rico, 100,000 people chanting "Inglés, no!" marched against prostatehood governor Pedro Rosselló's proposed law making English an official language on the island along with Spanish.[9]

Even while California's predominantly white voters were rejecting bilingualism, the state's educators were mandating a new multicultural curriculum. Once again these modest reforms ignited a firestorm of racial controversy. Demagogic academicians gained headlines with exaggerated statements slandering some "other" group. Nonetheless, the curriculum changes gradually progressed.

The conflict over bilingualism was part of a larger struggle for better education. Most Latinos support the multicultural curriculum, recently introduced in several states. They believe it will help to build self-esteem in young Latinos and educate every American about the diversity of the nation's peoples and cultures. They hope that a more meaningful curriculum will encourage their children to stay in school. High school dropout rates among Latinos had escalated to more than 50 percent in some cities.

On college campuses, Latino students also joined together to combat another effort to roll back gains made in the sixties and seventies, the hiring of a sprinkling of nonwhite faculty. In 1992 and 1993 thousands of University of California students, led by MECHA, marched to protest the University of California–Santa Barbara administration's failure to appoint the nation's pioneering Chicano historian Rodolfo Acuña as the campus's first full-time Chicano studies professor. Acuña had founded California State University-Northridge's famed Chicano Studies Department. Latinos have also sparked several

marches against tuition hikes and budget cuts that undermine poorer students' chances.

A spirit of internationalism infused the Latino
struggle for social justice during ongoing debates on three
issues: Puerto Rico's status, immigration, and international trade. A nonbinding referendum on Puerto Rico's
status was conducted in November 1993. Only island residents were allowed to officially vote, causing some grum-
bling among the 40 percent of Puerto Ricans who lived
on the mainland (2.7 million). Voters narrowly rejected
statehood and kept the island's "Commonwealth" status.

The immigration issue came to a head with the debates surrounding the 1986 passage of IRCA. As we saw
in Chapter 7, employers welcomed IRCA's fine-print
guarantees of contract labor. Employers also hoped to use
IRCA's stiff regulations against "illegals" to deport undocumented workers who advocated unions. Latina "illegals" working at Long Island City's S.T.C. Knitwear
learned this in 1993 when their employer reported those
who were union supporters to the INS.[10]

As a concession to Latino and other human rights activists, IRCA provided amnesty for any immigrant able to
prove continuous residence since 1982. But it was difficult to apply for amnesty. People who for years had been
trying to hide their presence now had to prove they had
been here all along! The amnesty conditions violated the
standard family reunification criterion of U.S. immigration policy. Children and spouses of an amnesty applicant
could not remain in the country if they arrived after 1982.
IRCA caused the breakup of thousands of families at the
very time leading politicians were calling for "a return to
family values." After a few years of vigorous Latino protests, the INS made the amnesty cutoff date for family
members 1988.[11]

Not surprisingly, after IRCA's passage, the INS
granted immediate amnesty to thousands of agricultural
workers who had returned to Mexico, making them avail-

able to break strikes or replace unionizing workers. By 1990, Latino activists were hauling employers to court, charging them with enslaving Mexicans.[12]

Human rights organizations like the Committee on Chicano Rights (CCR) have done more than criticize IRCA. They have put forward their own program, recommending unlimited amnesty for "illegals." They champion fair wages and union rights; the demilitarization of the U.S.-Mexico border and the disbanding of the Border Patrol; and an end to U.S. support for dictators that creates political refugees. On the illegals, a Catholic Church immigration expert notes that IRCA wastes taxpayers' money: "It would be far more cost effective in the long run to legalize [immediately] these [undocumented] people and allow them to work and contribute."[13]

After IRCA failed to resolve the immigration issue, several politicians got behind President George Bush's proposed North American Free Trade Agreement (NAFTA). They argued that by bringing Mexico, Canada, and the United States into a common market, conditions in Mexico would improve and the flow of immigrants northward would diminish. Many working people feared that since labor costs in Mexico were one seventh of those in the United States, NAFTA would encourage even more "runaway plants." By 1993 American companies already owned nearly 2,000 maquiladoras (assembly plants) in Mexico. Later in 1993, Congress narrowly approved NAFTA, but only after a bruising political battle.

Most Latino workers and labor activists opposed NAFTA. Latino politicians first supported it and then began joining the opposition.[14] A powerful campaign was launched against NAFTA that brought together grassroots environmentalist, peace, and labor organizations in all three countries. They became known as "citizen diplomats." The internationally famed San Diego–based Border Arts Workshop took its Cafe Urgente ("Emergency Cafe") on the road in 1991 to educate people on NAFTA.

127

Participants at the Buffalo, New York Cafe Urgente told how they had lost their jobs when employers moved to Mexico. Speakers strongly condemned NAFTA's failure to guarantee decent conditions for Mexican workers. They also expressed concern over environmental protection, notoriously lax along the U.S.-Mexico border. One of the proposed alternatives to NAFTA called for replacing it with a long-range, well-funded "continental development program" to rebuild all three nations' economies.[15]

While Latino activists were busy with defensive campaigns against IRCA and NAFTA, a few others went on the offensive to start something new. In the economic hard times that took place after the Vietnam War wound down, "union bashing" became fashionable. But blaming the nation's shrinking labor unions for the sputtering economy made no sense. Only one of every seven workers belonged to unions, down from one of three in the 1960s. *Labor costs of production had dropped,* as workers' real wages (what their dollars can buy) declined.

Some Latinos had not forgotten labor history. They knew that the long-ago cry of *Huelga!* had won better conditions for millions of workers. They took a page out of the history books and made efforts to organize new independent unions to mount an offensive on behalf of "undocumented workers." Prior to IRCA's passage, organizers succeeded in unionizing more than 40,000 undocumented in the Southwest, Florida, and Washington, bringing them into the independent American Federation of Workers (AFW). AFW won a surprising number of strikes and persuaded the AFL-CIO to instruct all of its affiliated unions to protect the undocumented against INS raids and other abuses.[16]

In the 1980s a new union of mostly Mexican migrants from Texas, the Farm Labor Organizing Committee (FLOC), won a prolonged strike in the Midwest against the Campbell Soup Company. When Campbell later threatened to move its Michigan operations to Sinaloa (Mexico), FLOC worked out a joint collective bargaining arrangement with its Sinaloan counterpart, the Mexican Farm Workers Union. In the Southwest, Latino workers founded the Border Agricultural Workers Union that won several more strikes.[17]

To organize the undocumented of course meant having to deal with *la migra* (the INS). In the mid-1980s Latino labor organizers sponsored protests that won pledges of noncooperation with the INS from police departments in Chicago, Santa Ana, San Jose, New York and other cities. In 1993, after the Rodney King verdict in Los Angeles, a Tucson jury acquitted an INS Border Patrol agent who had murdered an unarmed man fleeing across the border and had then tried to conceal the body. Latino outrage caused authorities to announce a new trial, this time for the agent's violation of the victim's civil rights. A 1993 report, "Frontier Justice," by the respected human rights organization Americas Watch condemned the U.S. Justice Department for failing to properly investigate hundreds of complaints of brutality against the Border Patrol.[18]

Picking up on the new energies generated by independent Latino activists, major labor unions like the United Steelworkers of America and the apparel industry's ILGWU began opening their doors a crack to "illegals." The steelworkers' union launched the unsuccessful strike at Morenci, Arizona (discussed in Chapter 3). At General Motors' largest West Coast plant, in Van Nuys, California, UAW Latino leaders organized "undocumented" Mexicans and built a community-wide coalition that kept the plant open for years against threatened closings. Also, at various subcontracting auto-parts plants, the UAW organized new unions among Latinos, including Salvadoran refugees.[19]

By 1985 a third of the Teamsters' Los Angeles membership were said to be undocumented. In 1991 the rank-and-file insurgent group Teamsters for a Democratic

Union (TDU) won the elections for leadership of the International Brotherhood of Teamsters with an anti-Mafia reform slate that included the first Latino ever to sit on the Teamsters' executive board.[20]

Among the most promising recruits for new labor unions were women. By AFL-CIO estimates, Latinas were entering the labor force at twice the rate of all U.S. women, and twice as many women workers as men supported labor unions. For some time Latina women had been igniting some of the nation's most important labor struggles, including the twenty-one-month strike against the Farah Clothing Company won in 1974. In 1991, Latinas and others struck Diamond Walnut in Texas. They demanded wage hikes after the company acknowledged its highest profits in history. When Diamond brought in permanent replacement workers, the victimized employees, some of them descendants of the Latinas who struck in the 1930s (see Chapter 3), launched a consumers' boycott against Diamond. Their mailings said "Can nuts, not people!" and called for a law to prohibit permanent replacement of striking workers.

In New York City a college dropout from Puerto Rico and former janitor of a nursing home, Dennis Rivera, helped lead a successful "save the union" campaign among health care workers. In 1989 he was elected president of the independent District 1199 of the national Drug, Hospital and Health Care Employees Union. The 100,000 members of 1199 are predominantly African American, Latino, and female. Noting that the AFL-CIO often "has more in common with the employers than with the rank and file," Rivera accelerated the unionization of the lowest-paid and fastest growing layers of health care employees—mostly women who worked in nursing homes, outpatient facilities, home health care organizations, and independent clinics.[21]

Women played a key role in yet another copper-mine strike in the Morenci area of Arizona. National Guardsmen had to be called out in the mid-1980s to quell a series of miners' strikes there protesting Phelps Dodge's attempts to bust their thirteen unions. When a court injunction barred strikers from the mine gates, women strike supporters mounted pickets and protests, creating scenes reminiscent of the film *Salt of the Earth* (see Chapter 5). Commented one Arizona policeman: "If we could just get rid of those broads, we'd have it made." The strike petered out, however, and Phelps Dodge shut down much of its production for good.[22]

What of the future? Few Latinos believe things will get better soon. But of one thing they are certain: their heritage of struggle for social justice will not die.

"If you listen real hard," they like to say, "once again, across the land, you might just hear, however distant and softly at first, the rising cry of:

"Huelga! Viva la causa!"

SOURCE NOTES

INTRODUCTION

1. Quoted in Rubén G. Rumbaut, "The Americans: Latin American and Caribbean Peoples in the United States," in Alfred Stepan, ed., *Americas* (New York: Oxford University Press, 1992), p. 279.

2. For a good explanation of how the word *Hispanic* came into being, see Rodolfo Acuña, *Occupied America: A History of Chicanos,* 3d ed. (New York: Harper & Row, 1988), pp. ix–xi, 139.

3. It is now common to spell such terms, when used as nouns, without the hyphen—Cuban American, African American, etc.—and this is the style used in this book. However, the description *hyphenated American* still applies even when the hyphen is eliminated for stylistic reasons.

4. This WASP basis for the dominant culture traces its roots back to the days when the nation was a British colony. Assimilation has always been defined by the ideology of "Anglo-conformity," that is, use of a common language, law, and religion from England. Many Hispanics do not approve of such a limited ethnocentric understanding of the word *American,* since they view all the Western Hemisphere as "America" and therefore all its inhabitants as "Americans." For more, see Milton M. Gordon, *Assimilation in American Life: The Role of Race, Religion, and National Origins* (New York: Oxford University Press, 1964).

5. Similarly, in this book we use *Indians, indigenous peoples,* and *Native Americans* interchangeably, again letting the context determine the usage.

6. Hispanics may already outnumber African Americans, depending on how many "undocumented immigrants" there are. Technically, a minority is a group either numerically smaller than the dominant one or with less power (as in the case of women). On a worldwide basis, of course, whites are a numerical minority.

7. Some Latinos are racially white, but because the word *white* usually refers to people of European descent we will use it to refer to them. According to the U.S. Census Bureau estimates, Hispanics number about 25 million—or more if uncounted persons and "undocumented immigrants" are taken into account (Puerto Rico's 3.5 million residents are not included). Nearly two thirds of Hispanics are U.S.-born. The majority are of Mexican descent (64 percent), followed by Puerto Ricans (12 percent), Central Americans (5 percent), and South Americans, Domini-

cans, and Cubans (about 4 percent each). About 2 percent are from Spain; and the rest are "other," reporting themselves as "Latino," "Hispano," or by some other name. For more, see U.S. Bureau of the Census Current Population Reports P23–183, *Hispanic Americans Today* (Washington, D.C.: U.S. Government Printing Office, 1993).

8. For details, see James D. Cockcroft, *Outlaws in the Promised Land* (New York: Grove, 1988), pp. 48–51.

9. James P. Shenton, *Ethnicity and Immigration* (Washington, D.C.: American Historical Association, 1990), p. 16.

CHAPTER 1

1. Quoted in Philip S. Foner, *The Spanish-Cuban-American War and the Birth of American Imperialism* (New York: Monthly Review Press, 1972), vol. 1, p. xxx.

2. Based on incident in Lisandro Pérez, "Cubans in the United States: The Paradoxes of Exile Culture," *Culturefront* (Winter 1993), pp. 15–16. For more on Ybor City, see *Encyclopedia of the American Left* (New York: Garland, 1990), pp. 863–64; Gary R. Mormino and George E. Pozzetta, *The Immigrant World of Ybor City: Italians and Their Latin Neighbors in Tampa, 1885–1985* (Urbana: University of Illinois Press, 1987).

3. Quoted in James D. Cockcroft, *Neighbors in Turmoil: Latin America* (New York: Harper & Row, 1989), pp. 78, 250 (rev. ed., Chicago: Nelson-Hall, 1995).

4. Ibid., p. 250.

5. Walter Lord, "Myths and Realities of the Alamo," *The American West*, V:3 (May 1968). For more on Mexico's independence and turbulent first decades as a republic, see James D. Cockcroft, *Mexico* (New York: Monthly Review Press, 1990), pp. 58–74.

6. Quoted in Rodolfo Acuña, *Occupied America: A History of Chicanos*, 3d ed. (New York: Harper & Row, 1988), p. 11.

7. Quoted in Cockcroft, *Neighbors*, p. 80, and Acuña, p. 13.

8. For details, see Hedda Garza, "St. Patrick's Hero-Traitors," *San Francisco Examiner-Chronicle*, March 11, 1990.

9. Acuña, p. 20.

10. Quoted in Cockcroft, *Neighbors*, p. 250.

11. For more on Martí and the exiles, see Gerald E. Poyo, *"With All, and for the Good of All": The Emergence of Popular Na-*

tionalism in the Cuban Communities of the United States, 1848–1898 (Durham: Duke University Press, 1989).

12. Quoted in Cockcroft, *Neighbors,* p. 251.

13. Ibid., p. 253.

14. Later testimonies by the leading Spanish general and other officials confirmed the fact that the guerrillas had already won the Spanish-Cuban War. See Cockcroft, *Neighbors,* p. 253.

15. Quoted in Howard Zinn, *A People's History of the United States* (New York: HarperPerennial, 1990), p. 302.

16. Quoted in Cockcroft, *Neighbors,* pp. 212, 253.

CHAPTER 2

1. Américo Paredes, *"With His Pistol in His Hand"* (Austin: University of Texas Press, 1958), p. 3.

2. Arthur Rockford Manby is a true character. Antonio T. Chacón is a composite one based on author's interviews with descendants of New Mexico's original settlers and similar interviews reported by Bruce Johansen and Roberto Maestas in their *El Pueblo* (New York: Monthly Review Press, 1983).

3. For fuller details, see Cary McWilliams, *North from Mexico* (New York: Greenwood Press, 1968), p. 118; Rodolfo Acuña, *Occupied America: A History of Chicanos,* 3d ed. (New York: Harper & Row, 1988), p. 59.

4. Howard Zinn, *A People's History of the United States* (New York: HarperPerennial, 1990), pp. 206–9.

5. Acuña, p. 94. For more, see Arnoldo De León, *They Called Them Greasers: Anglo Attitudes Towards Mexicans in Texas, 1821–1900* (Austin: University of Texas Press, 1983).

6. Acuña, p. 64. For more, see Robert J. Rosenbaum, *Mexicano Resistance in the Southwest* (Austin: University of Texas Press, 1981).

7. McWilliams, pp. 119–21.

8. Quoted in Acuña, p. 114.

9. Acuña, p. 119.

10. Richard Griswold del Castillo, *The Treaty of Guadalupe Hidalgo: A Legacy of Conflict* (Norman: University of Oklahoma Press, 1990), p. 73.

11. Quoted in Acuña, p. 46. See also David Montejano, *Anglos and Mexicans in the Making of Texas, 1836–1986* (Austin: University of Texas Press, 1987), p. 53.

12. *The Ballad of Gregorio Cortez* (film), 1983.

13. Walter Prescott Webb, quoted in Acuña, pp. 162–63.

14. *New York Times,* June 21, 1993.

CHAPTER 5

1. Quoted in M. B. Schnapper, *American Labor: A Pictorial Social History* (Washington, D.C.: Public Affairs Press, 1975), p. 146.

2. Quoted in James D. Cockcroft, *Outlaws in the Promised Land* (New York: Grove, 1988), p. 132.

3. Ibid., p. 64.

4. Much of the information contained in this chapter is drawn from Rodolfo Acuña, *Occupied America: A History of Chicanos,* 3d ed., (New York: Harper & Row, 1988).

5. Howard Zinn, *A People's History of the United States* (New York: Harper & Row, 1990), p. 267; Jeremy Brecher, *Strike!* (Boston: South End Press, 1972), p. 31.

6. Quoted in Carey McWilliams, *North from Mexico* (New York: Greenwood Press, 1968), p. 196.

7. Famed educator Booker T. Washington reportedly went to President Theodore Roosevelt and told him of the many African Americans willing to take up the tools of industry, but Roosevelt ignored the idea. On Reconstruction and attacks on African Americans, see Zinn, pp. 192–205.

8. Quoted in Acuña, p. 158.

9. Quoted in Kitty Calavita, *U.S. Immigration Law and the Control of Labor: 1820–1924* (Orlando, Fla: Academic Press, 1984), p. 49.

10. Hubert Howe Bancroft, *History of Arizona and New Mexico* (San Francisco: The History Co., 1889), quoted in Acuña, pp. 94–95.

11. Quoted in Jay J. Wagoner, *Arizona Territory, 1863–1912* (Tucson: University of Arizona Press, 1970), p. 387.

12. Quoted in Acuña, p. 98.

13. Quoted in James D. Cockcroft, *Intellectual Precursors of the Mexican Revolution* (Austin: University of Texas Press, 1968), p. 134.

14. Cockcroft, *Intellectual,* pp. 135–138; W. Dirk Raat, *Revoltosos: Mexico's Rebels in the United States, 1903–1923* (College Station: Texas A&M University Press, 1981), pp. 65–123; Marshall Trimble, *Arizona: A Panoramic History of a Frontier State* (Garden City, N.Y.: Doubleday, 1977), pp. 325–326.

15. Samuel Yellen, *American Labor Struggles, 1877–1934* (New York: Monad Press, 1936), p. 101. See also Carolyn Ashbaugh, *Lucy Parsons, American Revolutionary* (Chicago: Charles H. Kerr, 1976), pp. 78–103; Brecher, p. 51; Lucy E. Parsons, *Life of Albert R. Parsons with Brief History of the Labor Movement in America* (Chicago: Lucy E. Parsons, 1889).

16. Acuña, p. 174.

17. Quoted in Yellen, p. 221.

18. Chicano Communications Center, *450 Años del Pueblo Chicano: 450 Years of Chicano History in Pictures* (Albuquerque, N.M.: Chicano Communications Center, 1976), p. 96; Yellen, pp. 205–250; Zinn, pp. 346–349.

19. McWilliams, p. 197.

20. Acuña, p. 166.

21. Quoted in Dan Georgakas, *Solidarity Forever: The IWW Reconsidered* (Chicago: Lakeview Press, 1985), pp. 130–132, 234–235.

22. From Frankfurter's report to the president, quoted in McWilliams, p. 197.

23. Mari Jo Buhle, "Agrarian Radicalism," in *Encyclopedia of the American Left* (New York: Garland, 1990), p. 8.

24. For more on the revolving door, see Cockcroft, *Outlaws,* pp. 15–16, 42–93.

25. Georgakas, pp. 30–53.

26. The fined "prisoner" reportedly left the court with $47.50 in fifty-cent fines jingling in his pocket and "the light of Heaven" shining in his eyes. Quoted in B. A. Botkin, ed., *Sidewalks of America* (New York: Bobbs-Merrill, 1954), p. 442.

27. Acuña, p. 209.

28. For the story in the Midwest, see Dennis Nodín Valdés, *Al Norte* (Austin: University of Texas Press, 1990).

29. For more on the important role of women, see Hedda Garza, *Latinas: Hispanic Women in the United States* (New York: Franklin Watts, 1994); Vicki L. Ruiz, *Cannery Women, Cannery Lives: Mexican Women, Unionization, and the California Food Processing Industry, 1930–1950* (Albuquerque: University of New Mexico Press, 1987).

30. For more on these and other Latinas, see Garza; also, Mario T. García, *Mexican Americas* (New Haven, Conn.: Yale University Press, 1989), pp. 145–174.

31. For details, see Acuña, p. 229, and Schnapper, pp. 506–507.

CHAPTER 4

1. Both quotations from James D. Cockcroft, *Neighbors in Turmoil: Latin America* (New York: Harper & Row, 1989), pp. 168, 275 (rev. ed., Chicago: Nelson-Hall, 1995).

2. Quoted in *ibid.*, p. 282. For more on the Puerto Ricans in this period, see Francesco Cordasco and Eugene Bucchioni, eds.), *The Puerto Rican Experience* (Totowa, N.J.: Greenwood Press, 1984), pp. 15–42; Virginia E. Sánchez Korrol, *From Colonia to Community: The History of Puerto Ricans in New York City, 1917–1948* (Westport, Conn.: Greenwood Press, 1983).

3. Sánchez Korrol, p. 197.

4. Quoted in Cockcroft, p. 34.

5. Ibid., pp. 174, 254, 299.

6. Ibid., p. 254.

7. Carlos Feliciano, interview with author, 1973.

8. Conrad Lynn, *There Is a Fountain: The Autobiography of Conrad Lynn* (Brooklyn, N.Y.: Lawrence Hill Books, 1993), p. 126.

9. Edna Acosta-Belén, *The Puerto Rican Woman* (New York: Praeger, 1986), p. 14. On Operation Bootstrap, see Emilio Pantojas-Garcia, *Development Strategies as Ideology: Puerto Rico's Export-Led Industrialization Experience* (Boulder, Colo.: Lynne Rienner Publishers, 1990), pp. 16, 75, 88, 141–42.

10. Quoted in Jonathan C. Brown, "Foreign and Native-Born Workers in Porfirian Mexico," *American Historical Review,* June 1993, p. 790.

11. For the story on the *Magonistas* and the Mexican Revolution, see James D. Cockcroft, *Intellectual Precursors of the Mexican Revolution* (Austin: University of Texas Press, 1968); Juan Gómez Quiñones, *Sembradores, Ricardo Flores Magón y el Partido Liberal Mexicano: A Eulogy and Critique* (Los Angeles: Aztlán Publications, University of California, 1973); and W. Dirk Raat, *Revoltosos: Mexico's Rebels in the United States, 1903–1923* (College Station: Texas A & M University Press, 1981).

12. In line with the PLM's call for protection of Mexican immigrant workers against violations of their human rights, the Mexican Constitution's Article 123 prohibits the unregulated hiring of Mexican citizens for employment abroad—a clause often cited by

defenders of immigrant workers' human rights (see Chapters 5, 7, and 8). Earlier "precursor revolts" like Catarino Garza's in 1891 had less enduring impact than the PLM's. A Texas journalist and *mutualista,* Garza, with a thousand followers, carried out three unsuccessful raids into northern Mexico.

13. See Mary (Mother) Jones, *The Autobiography of Mother Jones* (Chicago: Charles H. Kerr, 1972), pp. 140–141.

14. For details, see Lowell L. Blaisdell, *The Desert Revolution: Baja California, 1911* (Madison: University of Wisconsin Press, 1962).

15. For a brief account of the Mexican Revolution, see James D. Cockcroft, *Mexico* (New York: Monthly Review Press, 1990), pp. 99–114. Later, Flores Magón was sentenced to twenty-one years in a U.S. prison for violation of the 1917 Espionage Act. The evidence was so flimsy that everyone knew the prominent Mexican freedom fighter was being railroaded along with Emma Goldman and other radicals of the time (Raat, pp. 275–290). Flores Magón died in Fort Leavenworth Prison in 1922, officially of cardiac arrest. Some suspected foul play. His name, like those of Villa and Zapata, is still held in reverence among Mexican-American advocates of social justice.

16. U.S. military officer Neill Macaulay later wrote an evenhanded account of the "dirty war": *The Sandino Affair* (New York: Quadrangle Books, 1967).

17. Quoted in James D. Cockcroft, *Daniel Ortega* (New York: Chelsea House, 1991), p. 35. Italics added.

18. For details, see Cockcroft, *Neighbors* pp. 102–119.

CHAPTER 5

1. Both quotations from Mario T. García, *Mexican Americans* (New Haven: Yale University Press, 1989), pp. 25, 222.

2. Quoted in Benjamin Márquez, *LULAC* (Austin: University of Texas Press, 1993), p. 32. See also Rodolfo Acuña, *Occupied America: A History of Chicanos* (New York: Harper & Row, 1988), pp. 239–241. For a history of LULAC through the 1980s, see Richard A. Garcia, *Rise of the Mexican American Middle Class,* pp. 252–322. For the 1929–1960 period see Mario T. García, pp. 25–61.

3. Quoted in Mario T. García, p. 31.

4. Theodore Lothrop Stoddard, *The Rising Tide of Labor Against White World-Supremacy* (New York: Scribner, 1920), pp.

107–108. Madden quote from Acuña, p. 186. On the use of eugenics, see Remsen Crawford, "The Menace of Mexican Immigration," *Current History*, 31:5 (1930), p. 905, and C. M. Goethe, "Other Aspects of the Problem," *Current History*, 28:5 (1928), p. 767.

5. Quoted in Mario T. García, p. 27.

6. Quoted in Carlos Vásquez and Manuel García y Griego, eds., *Mexican-U.S. Relations, Conflict and Convergence* (Los Angeles: UCLA Chicano Studies Research Center, 1983), p. 458.

7. For more, see Robert R. Alvarez, "National Politics and Local Responses: The Nation's First Successful School Desegregation Case," in Henry Trueba and Concha Delgado-Gaitan, eds., *Schooling and Society: Learning Content Through Culture* (New York: Praeger, 1988), pp. 37–52.

8. *Scribner's Commentary*, noted in James Jennings and Monte Rivera, eds., *Puerto Rican Politics in Urban America* (Westport, Conn.: Greenwood Press, 1984), p. 37.

9. For more, see Mario T. García, pp. 145–174; Joan Moore and Harry Pachon, *Hispanics in the United States* (Englewood Cliffs, N.J.: Prentice-Hall, 1985), pp. 177–178.

10. For details on Sleepy Lagoon and the zoot suit riots, see Carey McWilliams, *North from Mexico* (New York: Greenwood Press, 1968), pp. 228–258; Acuña, pp. 256–260; Mario T. García, pp. 171–173; Mauricio Mazón, *The Zoot-Suit Riots* (Austin: University of Texas Press, 1984). The maker of the 1981 film was Luis Valdés, who started out as a director and actor for the farm workers' El Teatro Campesino (see Chapter 6).

11. For more on segregation in the Armed Forces, see Hedda Garza, *Military Integration* (Franklin Watts, 1995).

12. For more on the Cold War, see James Aranson, *The Press and the Cold War* (Indianapolis: Bobbs-Merrill, 1970); Richard M. Freeland, *The Truman Doctrine and the Origins of McCarthyism* (New York: Knopf, 1971); Mary Beth Norton, *A People & A Nation* (Boston: Houghton Mifflin, 1984), pp. 434–435; Howard Zinn, *A People's History of the United States* (New York: HarperPerennial, 1990), pp. 416–418.

13. For more, see Acuña, pp. 294–295; Mario T. Garcia, pp. 56–58, 89–91.

14. For the full story, see Acuña, p. 292, and Mario T. García, pp. 49–51.

15. For more on the GI Forum, CSO, and other civil rights organizations, see Acuña, pp. 253, 283–293; Mario T. García, pp. 19, 101–103; Moore and Pachon, p. 178; Dennis Nodín Valdés, *El Pueblo Mexicano en Detroit y Michigan: A Social History* (Detroit: Wayne State University, 1982), pp. 75–77.

16. The McCarran-Walter Act was later defanged by amendments to immigration law. In its original form, it allowed for stripping naturalized citizens of their citizenship; excluded suspected "communists and subversives" from entering the country; and permitted the employment of undocumented aliens (so-called "Texas Proviso" on behalf of employers). ANMA also led a successful boycott against the Judy Canova radio show for its supposedly funny portrayal of Mexicans as lazy and stupid. For more on McCarran-Walter, ANMA, and Mine-Mill, see Acuña, pp. 234, 278–279; James D. Cockcroft, *Outlaws in the Promised Land*, (New York: Grove, 1988) pp. 73–75, 213–214; Mario T. García, pp. 199–227.

17. For details, see Mario T. García, pp. 167–173.

18. Quoted in Virginia E. Sánchez Korrol, *From Colonia to Community* (Westport, Conn.: Greenwood Press, 1983), p. 189. For more on El Barrio, see Gerald Meyer, *Vito Marcantonio: Radical Politician 1902–1954* (Albany: State University of New York Press, 1989), pp. 144–172.

19. The immigrants still call the Rio Grande the "Rio Bravo" (angry river) because, as one old-time bracero told this author: "It's gobbled up a lot of Mexicans. . . . It has a fish with a beak that bites you in the stomach and empties your guts. That fish is evil." See James D. Cockcroft, *Outlaws in the Promised Land* (New York: Grove, 1988), pp. 33–34.

20. Quoted in Cockcroft, *Outlaws,* p. 68. For a summation of the bracero program, see Kitty Calavita, *Inside the State: The Bracero Program, Immigration, and the I.N.S.* (New York: Routledge, 1992), pp. 1–17, and Cockcroft, *Outlaws* pp. 67–88.

21. For more on McCarthyism, see Zinn, pp. 422–428.

22. Another exception was the Catholic church–sponsored Caballeros de San Juan, an assimilationist community organization combatting racial discrimination against Chicago's 30,000 recently arrived Puerto Ricans. See Felix M. Padilla, *Puerto Rican Chicago* (Notre Dame, Ind.: University of Notre Dame Press, 1987), pp. 126–137. For more on the 1950s, see Catarino Garza, *Puerto Ricans in the U.S.: The Struggle for Freedom* (New York:

Pathfinder Press, 1977), pp. 14–15; Jennings and Rivera, pp. 43–46; Adalberto López and James Petras, eds., *Puerto Rico and Puerto Ricans* (New York: Wiley, 1974), pp. 313–451; Padilla, pp. 78–143.

CHAPTER 6

1. Quotations from Piri Thomas, *Down These Mean Streets* (New York: New American Library, 1967), and Rodolfo "Corky" Gonzales, *I Am Joaquín* (New York: Bantam Books, 1972).

2. Author's observation, June 1968.

3. For more, see Howard Zinn, *A People's History of the United States* (New York: Harper & Row, 1990), pp. 435–528.

4. Hedda Garza, *Joan Baez* (New York: Chelsea House, 1991), pp. 26–29.

5. On Huerta and other UFW women, see Rosalyn Baxandall, Linda Gordon, and Susan Reverby, eds., *America's Working Women* (New York: Random House, 1976), pp. 363–372; and Hedda Garza, *Latinas: Hispanic Women in the United States* (New York: Franklin Watts, 1994). On Chavez and the UFW, see James D. Cockcroft, *Outlaws in the Promised Land* (New York: Grove, 1988), pp. 179–189; John Gregory Dunne, *Delano* (New York: Farrar, Straus, 1967); and Consuelo Rodriguez, *Cesar Chavez* (New York: Chelsea House, 1991).

6. Cited in Joan Moore and Harry Pachon, *Hispanics in the United States* (Englewood Cliffs, N.J.: Prentice-Hall, 1985), p. 181. See also Armando B. Rendon, *Chicano Manifesto* (New York: Macmillan, 1971), pp. 119–131. Gonzales's epic poem *I Am Joaquín* inspired Mexican Americans the way Pedro Pietri's poem *Puerto Rican Obituary* and ex-convict Piri Thomas's novel *Down These Mean Streets* inspired U.S.-born Puerto Ricans.

7. *Chicano* was a term used by the working class to refer to itself, but middle-class people often used it to put down the lower class. See Rodolfo Acuña, *Occupied America: A History of Chicanos*, 3d ed. (New York: Harper & Row, 1988), p. ix.

8. For details, see John Staples Shockley, *Chicago Revolt in a Texas Town* (Notre Dame, Ind.: University of Notre Dame Press, 1974), pp. 1–2, 111–149.

9. Quoted in Gilberto López y Rivas, *The Chicanos* (New York: Monthly Review Press, 1973), p. 167. For more on Chicana women in the Brown Berets, see Garza, *Latinas*.

10. On "blowouts" and MECHA, see Carlos Muñoz, Jr., *Youth, Identity, Power* (New York: Verso, 1989), pp. 64–97.

11. "Cosmo" quote from Frank Browning, "From Rumble to Revolution: The Young Lords," in Francesco Cordasco and Eugene Bucchioni, eds., *The Puerto Rican Experience* (Totowa, N.J.: Rowman and Littlefield, 1973), p. 233; gang mural reproduced in Eva Cockcroft, John Weber, and James Cockcroft, *Toward a People's Art: The Contemporary Mural Movement* (New York: Dutton, 1977), color plate 8. For more on the Young Lords, see Cordasco and Bucchioni, pp. 231–275; Catarino Garza, ed., *Puerto Ricans in the U.S.* (New York: Pathfinder Press, 1977), pp. 42–43; Felix M. Padilla, *Puerto Rican Chicago,* pp. 117–123; Clara E. Rodríguez, Virginia Sanchez Korrol, and Jose Oscar Alers, eds., *The Puerto Rican Struggle: Essays on Survival in the U.S.* (Maplewood, N.J.: The Waterfront Press, 1980), pp. 121–128. On Chicago gangs, see note 19.

12. Author's interviews with Young Lords minister of information Tony Báez, June 1971.

13. For the complete YLP Program, see Cordasco and Bucchioni, pp. 271–275. Young Lord leaders included several women (see Cordasco and Bucchioni, pp. 231–232, 252–253), as well as occasional young Puerto Rican *independistas* fleeing repression on the island. Most Young Lords, like almost half the mainland Puerto Ricans by then, were born in the United States.

14. That same year the Puerto Rican Socialist Party rallied Latinos and others to the cause of Carlos Feliciano, the friend of Albizu Campos. Charged with terrorist bombings, Feliciano was held in a New York City jail for seventeen months before coming to trial. The jury acquitted Feliciano when it decided that he was the victim of a police frame-up. See William M. Kunstler, "Introduction," in *Carlos Feliciano: History and Repression* (New York: Committee to Defend Carlos Feliciano, 1972), pp. 3–4.

15. For more complete information, see Hedda Garza, *Latinas.*

16. For more, see Hedda Garza, *Latinas,* and Frances Fox Piven and Richard A. Cloward, *Poor People's Movements* (New York: Vintage Books, 1979), pp. 264–359.

17. Quoted in Padilla, p. 147. For a list of New Jersey riots, see Francesco Cordasco, ed., *The Puerto Ricans 1493–1973* (Dobbs Ferry, N.Y.: Oceana Publications, 1973), p. 13. Even in barrios where Latinos elected Republicans and were uninvolved with mili-

144

tant groups of the sixties, trouble came. For example, Dallas police assaulted a peaceful march of local Latinos and African-American families seeking justice against a policeman who had shot a twelve-year-old Mexican-American boy in the back of the head while holding him at a precinct. The boy had refused to confess to a burglary he had not committed. See Shirley Achor, *Mexican Americans in a Dallas Barrio* (Tucson: University of Arizona Press, 1978), pp. 106–108, 148–153.

18. See Barry Bluestone and Bennett Harrison, *The Deindustrialization of America* (New York: Basic Books, 1982).

19. Achor, pp. 105–106; New York State Department of Correctional Services, *Hispanic Inmate Task Force* (New York: 1986), p. 6. For information on how gangs change, see Mary G. Harris, *Cholas Latino Girls and Gangs* (New York: AMS Press, 1988), pp. 166–198; John M. Hagedorn, *People and Folks* (Chicago: Lake View Press, 1988), pp. 131–170; Joan W. Moore, *Homeboys and Homegirls in Change* (Philadelphia: Temple University Press, 1991), pp. 45–104; Felix M. Padilla, *The Gang as an American Enterprise* (New Brunswick, N.J.: Rutgers University Press, 1992), pp. 117–187; James Diego Vigil, *Barrio Gangs* (Austin: University of Texas Press, 1988), pp. 24–34.

20. Quoted in Zinn, p. 511.

21. Acuña, p. 346; *Hispanic,* August 1993, p. 36.

22. Acuña, pp. 346–350.

23. For more on this pattern, see Susan Faludi, *Backlash* (New York: Crown, 1991); Hedda Garza, *Latinas;* Edwin Melendez, Clara Rodriguez and Janis Barry Figueroa, eds., *Hispanics in the Labor Force* (New York: Plenum Press, 1991), pp. 6–20; Rebecca Morales and Frank Bonilla, eds., *Latinos in a Changing U.S. Economy* (Newbury Park, Calif.: Sage Publications, 1993), pp. 1–36, 91; Felix M. Padilla, *Latino Ethnic Consciousness* (Notre Dame, Ind.: University of Notre Dame Press, 1985), pp. 84–118; Clara E. Rodríguez, *Puerto Ricans Born in the U.S.A.* (Boston: Unwin Hyman, 1989), pp. 87–89.

24. Pablo "Yoruba" Guzmán, "Puerto Rican Barrio Politics in the United States," in Rodríguez, Sanchez Korrol, and Alers, pp. 127–128.

25. Richard Griswold del Castillo, *The Treaty of Guadalupe Hidalgo: A Legacy of Conflict* (Norman: University of Oklahoma Press, 1990), p. 144.

26. See, for example, Robert J. Goldstein, *Political Repression in Modern America, from 1870 to Present* (Cambridge, Mass.: Schenkman, 1978), p. 429. See also, Acuña, pp. 342–344, 350–352; Zinn, pp. 453, 455. Occasional lawsuits against the authorities' illegal actions were won many years later, including the Hampton case. In 1984 the Spanish Action Community of Chicago (SACC) won a class action suit against the Chicago Police Department for its violations of civil rights that all but destroyed SACC at the height of its power in 1966—see Padilla, *Puerto Rican Chicago,* pp. 165–179, 250. Even the 1968 Civil Rights Act was used to send people off to jail—for using interstate facilities such as the phone or mail to "encourage a riot."

CHAPTER 7

1. Quoted in Eugenia Georges, *The Making of a Transnational Community: Migration, Development, and Cultural Change in the Dominican Republic* (New York: Cambridge University Press, 1990), p. 225.

2. Quoted in Rodolfo Rodríguez Zaldívar and Bienvenido Madan, *Golden Pages of the Cuban Exiles, 1959–1983* (self-published), p. 148.

3. For the full story, see in Ann Crittenden, *Sanctuary* (New York: Weidenfeld & Nicolson, 1988).

4. Quoted in Crittenden, p. 336.

5. Ibid., p. 338.

6. Ibid., pp. 162, 338.

7. The other two were family reunification and skills needed in the U.S. economy.

8. James D. Cockcroft, *Neighbors in Turmoil: Latin American* (New York: Harper & Row, 1989), pp. 60–61 (rev. ed., Chicago: Nelson-Hall, 1995); and James D. Cockcroft, *Outlaws in the Promised Land* (New York: Grove, 1988), pp. 173, 242–252.

9. Some were frightened teenagers avoiding the military draft introduced by the government to fend off the contra invasion. The 1990 Census counted 203,000 Nicaraguans. For more, see James D. Cockcroft, *Daniel Ortega* (New York: Chelsea House, 1991), pp. 75–97; Crittenden, p. 21; Joe Vidueira, "Miami, Mi Amigo: Nicaraguans in the Magic City," *Hispanic* (September 1993), pp. 68–72.

10. For more, see note 8 and Cockcroft, *Daniel Ortega,* p. 93.

11. A 1993 UN Truth Commission report confirmed what movement activists had been saying all along. Sixty-two Salvadoran military officers were responsible for village massacres, the rape and murder of four U.S. churchwomen, and the murders of several priests and Archbishop Oscar Romero. Forty-seven of the sixty-two were graduates of the U.S. Army School of the Americas, now in Fort Benning, Georgia.

12. The phrasing is the author's. For details, see Cockcroft, *Neighbors,* almost any chapter.

13. Rebecca Morales and Frank Bonilla, eds., *Latinos in a Changing U.S. Economy* (Newbury Park: Sage Publications, 1993), p. 104. For more, see Cockcroft, *Neighbors,* pp. 294–310; James Ferguson, *The Dominican Republic* (London: The Latin American Bureau, 1992), pp. 75–81; Nancy Foner, ed., *New Immigrants in New York* (New York: Columbia University Press, 1987), pp. 103–126; Georges, pp. 81–123; Sherri Grasmuck and Patricia R. Pessar, *Between Two Islands* (Berkeley: University of California Press, 1991), pp. 98–208.

14. Quoted in Hedda Garza, *Salvador Allende* (New York: Chelsea House, 1989), p. 15.

15. For further information, see Cockcroft, *Neighbors,* p. 52, pp. 211–226; Independent Commission of Inquiry on the U.S. Invasion of Panama, *The U.S. Invasion of Panama: Operation Just Cause* (Boston: South End Press, 1991); George Priestley, *Military Government and Popular Participation in Panama* (Boulder, Colo.: Westview Press, 1986).

16. Quoted in Rodríguez Zaldívar and Madan, p. 148.

17. Author's interviews with Cuban Americans working for *Areito.* See also *Culturefront,* 2:1 (Winter 1993), p. 21; Joan Didion, *Miami* (New York: Simon and Schuster, 1987), pp. 116–125.

18. Quoted in Octavio Emilio Nuiry, "King of the Barrio," *Hispanic,* April 1993, p. 32. See also M. Patricia Fernández Kelly and Alejandro Portes, "Continent on the Move: Immigrants and Refugees in the Americas," in Alfred Stepan, ed., *Americas* (New York: Oxford University Press, 1992), pp. 269–270.

19. Author's interviews with Salvadoran refugees, August 1993.

20. *New York Times,* January 19, 1992.

21. Cockcroft, *Outlaws,* p. 254; Morales and Bonilla, p. 92.

22. Hispanic organizations like LULAC, MALDEF, the GI Forum, the Cuban National Planning Council, and the San Diego-based Committee on Chicano Rights (CCR) initially mounted strong opposition to IRCA but later divided. See Cockcroft, *Outlaws*, pp. 141, 209–238, 283. For more, see Frank D. Bean, Barry Edmonston, and Jeffrey S. Passel, *Undocumented Immigration to the United States* (Washington, D.C.: Urban Institute Press, 1990), pp. 222–225.

23. A 1993 research report to the Ford Foundation attributed the increased number of "hate crimes" to a shrinking job market. See Robert L. Bach et al., *Changing Relations* (New York: Ford Foundation, 1993).

24. Soon the detainees were back at work (Cockcroft, Outlaws, p. 41). Researchers have discovered that, on balance, immigrants actually contribute to job creation rather than to job loss—see, for example, Thomas Muller and Thomas J. Espenshade, *The Fourth Wave* (Washington, D.C.: Urban Institute Press, 1985), pp. 91–122, 145–156.

25. Ford Foundation, *Hispanics: Challenges and Opportunities* (New York: 1984), p. 20. For more on the immigrants' contributions to the economy, see Cockcroft, *Outlaws*, pp. 115–150; Gregory DeFreitas, *Inequality at Work* (New York: Oxford University Press, 1991), pp. 209–231, 248–251; and note 24.

26. A bone-chilling compilation of media distortions may be found in Celestino Fernandez, "The Border Patrol and News Media Coverage of Undocumented Mexican Immigration During the 1970s," *California Sociologist*, 5 (1982). See also Rodolfo Acuña, *Occupied America: A History of Chicanos* (New York: HarperCollins, 1988), pp. 371–376.

27. Committee on Chicano Rights (CCR), *A Chicano Perspective on the President's Immigration Proposals* (National City, Calif.: CCR, 1981). For the Bill of Rights text, see Cockcroft, *Outlaws*, pp. 281–282.

28. Author's interviews with attorney Peter Schey, 1981, 1987.

29. For the police messages and statement by Christopher, see *New York Times*, July 10, 1991.

30. Quoted in *New York Times*, June 5, 1991.

31. Tomás Rivera Center, "Latinos and the Los Angeles Uprising: The Economic Context," March 14, 1993, as reported in *The Latino Journal* (SUNY-Albany), March-April, 1993; Nuiry,

pp. 26–32; *New York Times,* May 29, 1992; author's interviews with Chicano human rights activists, June 1992.

CHAPTER 8

1. Quoted in Francesco Cordasco, ed., *The Puerto Ricans 1493–1973* (Dobbs Ferry, N.Y.: Oceana Publications, 1973), p. 82.

2. Author's observations, San Diego State University.

3. *Diálogo* (newsletter of National Puerto Rican Policy Network, Summer 1993), pp. 11–12.

4. Harry Pachon and Louis DeSipio, "Latino Elected Officials in the 1990s," *PS: Political Science and Politics,* June 1992, p. 213. Joan Moore and Harry Pachon, *Hispanics in the United States* (Englewood Cliffs, N.J.: Prentice-Hall, 1985), pp. 169–199.

5. *New York Times,* June 29, 1993.

6. James D. Cockcroft, *Neighbors in Turmoil: Latin America* (New York: Harper & Row, 1989), p. 292, (rev. ed. Chicago: Nelson Hall, 1994); Paul M. Ong and Evelyn Blumenberg, "An Unnatural Trade-Off: Latinos and Environmental Justice," in Rebecca Morales and Frank Bonilla, eds., *Latinos in a Changing U.S. Economy* (Newbury Park, CA: Sage Publications, 1993), pp. 210–222.

7. For details, see post-1987 issues of UFW's monthly *Food and Justice* and UFW video *The Wrath of Grapes.*

8. Quoted in Linda Chavez, *Out of the Barrio* (New York: Basic Books, 1991), p. 163. Chavez argues that multicultural programs so far have overemphasized building self-esteem through tracing one's Latino "roots" instead of assimilation into the dominant culture. On bilingual education's successes and failures, see Edward M. Chen, "Today's Immigrants Learn English as Fast as Yesterday's Did," *New York Times,* September 29, 1989, citing a 1985 Rand Corporation study and other research.

9. *New York Times,* January 25, May 23, 1993.

10. Ibid., June 15, 1993.

11. James D. Cockcroft, *Outlaws in the Promised Land* (New York: Grove, 1988), pp. 254–255; Annette Fuentes, "Immigration 'reform': Heaviest burden on women," reprint from *Listen Real Loud* (American Friends Service Committee, 1986).

12. *New York Times,* April 29, 1990; Cockcroft, *Outlaws,* p. 255.

13. Gilbert Carrasco of the U.S. Catholic Conference Mi-

gration and Refugee Services, quoted in Cockcroft, *Outlaws*, p. 257.

14. *New York Times*, October 12, 1993.

15. Author's participation at *Cafe Urgente*, Hall Walls, Buffalo, N.Y., August 16, 1991. A National Toxics Campaign Fund study concluded in 1991 that *maquiladoras* are "turning the border into a 2,000-mile-long Love Canal," while an American Medical Association report called the region "a virtual cesspool and breeding ground for infectious disease." For more on NAFTA, see John Cavanagh et al., eds., *Trading Freedom: How Free Trade Affects Our Lives, Work, and Environment* (San Francisco: Food First Books, 1992); Annette Fuentes, "Bad Table Manners: Latinos and NAFTA," *Diálogo* (Summer 1993), pp. 1–9; Nora Lustig et al., eds., *North American Free Trade: Assessing the Impact* (Washington, D.C.: Brookings Institution, 1992); Kim Moody and Mary McGinn, *Unions and Free Trade: Solidarity vs. Competition* (Detroit: Labor Notes, 1992).

16. For details, see Cockcroft, *Outlaws*, pp. 175–208.

17. For more, see W. K. Barger and Ernesto M. Reza, *The Farm Labor Movement in the Midwest* (Austin: University of Texas Press, 1993); Cockcroft, *Outlaws*, pp. 190–208; Kim Moody and Mary McGinn, *Unions and Free Trade: Solidarity vs. Competition* (Detroit: Labor Notes, 1992), p. 50; Kent Paterson, "Farmworkers," *Coatimundi* (Albuquerque, N.M.) 2:3 (Summer 1987), p. 16.

18. Cockcroft, *Outlaws*, p. 201; *Washington Post*, May 14, 1993; *New York Times*, May 31, 1992.

19. Cockcroft, *Outlaws*, pp. 140, 198–208.

20. Cockcroft, *Outlaws*, p. 200; Phil Kwik, "The Teamsters Victory: A Successful Strategy for Revitalizing the Labor Movement," *New Politics* 4:1 (Summer 1992), p. 155.

21. Quotations from Sam Roberts, "A New Face for American Labor," *New York Times Magazine*, May 10, 1992, p. 14. See also, *New York Times*, May 25, 1993. Even when culturally and linguistically isolated, Latinos continued to fight for labor's rights. In white, affluent suburban Chester County thirty miles west of Philadelphia some of the 4,000 Mexican workers in the "mushroom capital of the world" went on strike in 1993 and won the right to hold a union election (*Miami Herald*, May 23, 1993).

22. Later, jury verdicts and out-of-court settlements awarded half a million dollars to some of the strikers and their unions as compensation for violations of their constitutional rights.

Today, the nation's largest surviving copper mine at Morenci is operated by nonunion workers who steer clear of Clifton because of hostility from striker families who live there. Computers of Phelps Dodge and its Japanese partners run the equipment and keep track of every steam shovel. For more, see *Guardian,* June 13, 1990, p. 19; Barbara Kingsolver, *Holding the Line: Women in the Great Arizona Mine Strike of 1983* (Ithaca, N.Y.: ILR Press, Cornell University, 1989), pp. ix, 192–195; *New York Times,* March 19, 23, 1986.

BIBLIOGRAPHY

* An asterisk denotes books especially recommended for students.

Acosta-Belén, Edna, and Barbara R. Sjostrom, eds. *The Hispanic Experience in the United States.* New York: Praeger, 1986.

*Acuña, Rodolfo. *Occupied America: A History of Chicanos,* 3d ed. New York: Harper & Row, 1988.

*Chicano Communications Center. *450 Anos del Pueblo Chicano: 450 Years of Chicano History in Pictures.* Albuquerque, N.M.: Chicano Communications Center, 1976.

*Cockcroft, James D. *Neighbors in Turmoil: Latin America.* New York: Harper & Row, 1989. Rev. ed., Chicago: Nelson-Hall, 1995.

_____. *Outlaws in the Promised Land.* New York: Grove, 1988.

Cordasco, Francesco, and Eugene Bucchioni, eds. *The Puerto Rican Experience.* Totowa, N.J.: Rowman and Littlefield, 1973.

Crittenden, Ann. *Sanctuary.* New York: Weidenfeld & Nicolson, 1988.

*Ford Foundation. *Hispanics: Challenges and Opportunities.* New York: Ford Foundation, 1984.

García, Mario T. *Mexican Americans.* New Haven, Conn.: Yale University Press, 1989.

Garcia, Richard A. *Rise of the Mexican American Middle Class.* College Station: Texas A&M University Press, 1991.

*Garza, Hedda. *Latinas: Hispanic Women in the United States.* New York: Franklin Watts, 1994.

Georges, Eugenia. *The Making of a Transnational Community: Migration, Development, and Cultural Change in the Dominican Republic.* New York: Columbia University Press, 1990.

Grasmuck, Sherri, and Patricia R. Pessar. *Between Two Islands.* Berkeley: University of California Press, 1991.

Griswold del Castillo, Richard. *The Treaty of Guadalupe Hidalgo: A Legacy of Conflict.* Norman: University of Oklahoma Press, 1990.

*Leggett, John C., ed. *Mining the Fields: Farm Workers Fight Back.* Highland Park, N.J.: Raritan Institute, 1991.

Márquez, Benjamin. *LULAC.* Austin: University of Texas Press, 1993.

McWilliams, Carey. *North from Mexico.* New York: Greenwood Press, 1968.

*Moore, Joan, and Harry Pachon. *Hispanics in the United States.* Englewood Cliffs, N.J.: Prentice-Hall, 1985.

Muñoz, Carlos, Jr. *Youth, Identity, Power.* New York: Verso, 1989.

Padilla, Felix M. *Latino Ethnic Consciousness.* Notre Dame, Ind.: University of Notre Dame Press, 1985.

——————. *Puerto Rican Chicago.* Notre Dame, Ind.: University of Notre Dame Press, 1987.

Paredes, Américo. *"With His Pistol in His Hand."* Austin: University of Texas Press, 1958.

Portes, Alejandro, and Robert L. Bach. *Latin Journey.* Berkeley: University of California Press, 1985.

Poyo, Gerald E. *"With All, and for the Good of All".* Durham, N.C.: Duke University Press, 1989.

Prohias, Rafael J., and Lourdes Casal. *The Cuban Minority in the U.S.* New York: Arno Press, 1980.

Rodríguez, Clara E., Virginia Sánchez Korrol, and José Oscar Alers, eds. *The Puerto Rican Struggle: Essays on Survival in the U.S.* Maplewood, N.J.: The Waterfront Press, 1980.

Sánchez Korrol, Virgina E. *From Colonia to Community.* Westport, Conn.: Greenwood Press, 1983.

*Schnapper, M. B. *American Labor: A Pictorial Social History.* Washington, D.C.: Public Affairs Press, 1975.

Stepan, Alfred, ed. *Americas.* New York: Oxford University Press, 1992.

U.S. Bureau of the Census Current Population Reports P23–183. *Hispanic Americans Today.* Washington, D.C.: U.S. Government Printing Office, 1993.

*Zinn, Howard. *A People's History of the United States.* New York: Harper & Row, 1990.

FILMS AND VIDEOS

Año Nuevo. On "undocumented" farmworkers' unionizing.
"Ballad of an Unsung Hero"
The Ballad of Gregorio Cortez. On famed "social bandit."
El Norte. On Guatemalan refugees in the United States.
Growing up Hispanic.
Here to Stay: Young Immigrants from El Salvador.
Latino. On a Chicano training the contras.
Los Sures. On a Brooklyn barrio.
Manos a la Obra: The Story of Operation Bootstrap.
The Nine Nations of North America: Mexamerica. PBS, 1988.
Our Hispanic Heritage.
The Panama Deception. 1992 Oscar winner.
Portrait of Castro's Cuba. PBS, 1991. Narrator James Earl Jones.
Puerto Rico: A Colony the American Way.
Salt of the Earth. On famous strike and women's victory.
Who's Running This War? PBS, 1986. On Central American warfare.
Yo Soy (I Am). On Chicanos.
Zoot Suit. On anti-Mexican American race riots.

INDEX

DATE DUE
